PETROLEUM V. NASBY
(DAVID ROSS LOCKE)

by **JAMES C. AUSTIN**
Southern Illinois University

 89

Twayne Publishers, Inc.   ::   New York

MANUFACTURED IN THE UNITED STATES OF AMERICA BY
UNITED PRINTING SERVICES, INC.
NEW HAVEN, CONN.

To
W. M. AUSTIN
who won't agree

PETROLEUM V. NASBY

by

James C. Austin

David Ross Locke, known as Petroleum Vesuvius Nasby to newspaper readers of the Civil War era and later, was the most effective political satirist of his time. Writer of "comic" letters to the newspapers, Locke depicted himself as a dishonest political hack who swilled whisky, hated Negroes, and all in all embodied what his creator hated most in contemporary society. Actually, as a prominent editor, Locke agitated for reforms that led to five amendments to the Constitution of the United States, and he was publicly cited by Lincoln, Grant, and Hayes for his journalistic support.

When he died of consumption at the age of fifty-five, David Ross Locke wanted to be remembered as a public benefactor and as a writer of hymns. He remains as Petroleum V. Nasby of the "comic" letters. But it is wrong to associate him with such humorists as Artemus Ward and Josh Billings. His appeal was rooted in a fierce moral indignation, and he created Petroleum Nasby to underscore the bigotry and political corruption of the Civil War era, the Reconstruction, and the Gilded Age.

Preface

WHEN I BEGAN THIS BOOK, Petroleum V. Nasby was out of print except for brief selections in anthologies. In 1962, Harvey S. Ford edited a pamphlet of *Civil War Letters of Petroleum V. Nasby,* and in 1963, Joseph Jones did an abridged edition of *The Struggles of Petroleum V. Nasby.* The Civil War and Negro rights are issues today as they were in Nasby's time, and the voice of Nasby is not yet utterly silenced.

David Ross Locke, the newspaperman who made Nasby into such a pungent character that the public confused him with his author, was a satirist—not a humorist. In his voluminous writing, he pounded again and again and again at the evils he saw before him in the gilded society of his day. And, from all indications, he got results. I wish he could be so effective today.

As soon as I began to examine the documents concerning Locke's life, I discovered that almost everything that has been printed about him is touched with myth. Even his own accounts, written generally for promotional purposes, are subject to question. The one published book about Locke, *Petroleum Vesuvius Nasby* (1936), by the genial Cyril Clemens, relies necessarily on many of these unscholarly accounts.

The purpose of my book is analytical rather than biographical. I have tried to give the reader an overall view of Locke's works, their techniques, and their values. For this reason, and because Locke's works are not readily available, I have quoted extensively from both his collected writings and from those that have never been republished since their original appearance in newspapers and magazines. I hope too that I have laid a groundwork for future biographical studies. But I do not claim to have dispelled all the myth. I have based my biographical statements on original documents whenever possible—manuscripts, news reports, and the immediate reactions of firsthand witnesses. But I suspect that there remain some errors, both in fact and in interpretation. The correction of these errors is left to the biographical researches of John M. Harrison.

To Professor Harrison I want to devote a paragraph. My acquaintance with him has been through his work and through the United States mail. But it has been the most refreshing instance of the community of scholars that I have had the honor to experience. Not only did he freely answer my many questions, pertinent and impertinent, but he offered the use of some of his own notes and specific researches. I mean in no way to implicate him in the errors of this book. But insofar as I accomplish my purpose—to present David Ross Locke and his works in the most objective and practicable light—Mr. Harrison is in large part responsible. I look forward to the publication of Harrison's biography of Locke. Until then, Locke's significance in the history of American journalism—with all its ramifications—can only be suggested.

I wish also to acknowledge the assistance of a good many librarians and specialists in photo-duplication. Without these unsung heroes, modern research could not be what it is. Mrs. Elizabeth Martin, Librarian of the Ohio Historical Society, was more than generous with her time and effort in putting up with my requests. The growing collection of Ohio newspapers at the Historical Society will be of inestimable value to future researches. I am grateful also to Mrs. Irene McCreery, Head of the Local History and Genealogy Division of the Toledo Public Library; to Mr. Watt P. Marchman and Mrs. Ruth E. Ballenger of The Rutherford B. Hayes Library; to Miss Ruth N. Kerr of The Bucyrus Public Library; to Mr. Edwin L. Heminger of the Findlay, Ohio, *Republican-Courier;* to Miss Lois MacKellar and Mr. A. T. Dickinson, Jr., of the Mansfield Public Library; and to Mrs. Dorothea B. Jackson, Executive Secretary of the Cortland County Historical Society. I am happy also to acknowledge the assistance of Mrs. William Kutter and of the Humanities Division and the Faculty Research Committee of Southern Illinois University, Edwardsville Campus.

JAMES C. AUSTIN

Collinsville, Illinois

Contents

Chapter

Chronology   11

1. Rags to Riches   19

2. Of Slaves and Presidents   44

3. The Reverse Logic of Petroleum V. Nasby   64

4. Belles Lettres   99

5. Teller of Tales   120

   Notes and References   141

   Selected Bibliography   148

   Index   157

Chronology

1833   David Ross Locke was born, Vestal, Broome County, New York, September 20.

1845   Apprenticed to Cortland, New York, *Democrat*.

1850   Edited unsuccessfully the Corning, New York, *Fountain of Temperance*.

1851   Became reporter, then assistant editor, for Pittsburgh *Chronicle*.

1853   Became publisher and editor, with James G. Robinson, of the Plymouth, Ohio, *Advertiser*, October 22.

1855   Married Martha H. Bodine, March 7. Left the *Advertiser*, October 6. Became editor and proprietor, with Robinson and Roeliff Brinkerhoff, of the Mansfield, Ohio, *Herald*, September 12.

1856   Left the *Herald*, January 30. Robinson Locke was born March 15. D. R. Locke became editor and publisher of the Bucyrus, Ohio, *Journal*, March 20.

1860   Published "Secession in a New Spot," which later became the opening Nasby letter, December 13, Bucyrus *Journal*.

1861   Commissioned Second Lieutenant, Sixty-Fifth Infantry, November 5. Left the *Journal*, November 8. Became owner December 13, and editor December 27, of the Findlay, Ohio, *Hancock Jeffersonian*.

1862   Wrote first Nasby letter, *Hancock Jeffersonian*, April 25.

1864   Published *The Nasby Papers*.

1865   Left *Jeffersonian*, February 10. Worked on Bellefontaine, Ohio, *Republican*. Became editor of Toledo *Blade*, October 15.

1866   Published *Divers Views* and *Androo Johnson*.

1867   Became partner in A. D. Pelton & Company, owners of the *Blade*. Published *Swingin' Round the Cirkle*. Met Thomas Nast. Delivered "Cussid Be Canaan" in Boston, December 22.

1868   Published *Ekkoes from Kentucky* and *The Impendin Crisis*. Delivered "The Struggles of a Conservative with the Woman Question" in Boston, December 16.

1869   Met Samuel Clemens, March.

1870   Contributed to founding of *The Index*, beginning January 1. Delivered "In Search of the Man of Sin" in Boston, December 29.

1871   Probably began connection with the New York *Evening Mail*.

1872   Published *The Struggles*.

1873   Promoted Yost's "Type Writer." Lectured in New York City, November 18. Helped organize Blade Printing & Paper Company in December.

1874   Became president of Blade Printing, March.

1875   Published *The Morals of Abou Ben Adhem* and *Inflation at the Cross Roads*.

1876   *Inflation* was performed. Became owner and president Toledo Blade Company.

1877   Published *The President's Policy*.

1879   *Widow Bedott* was performed in Providence, Rhode Island, about January 31. Published *A Paper City*.

1880   *Widow Bedott* opened in New York City, March 15. Published *The Democratic John Bunyan*.

1881   Published *The Diary of an Office Seeker*. Began European tour, spring.

1882   Published *Hannah Jane* and *Nasby in Exile*.

1884   Incorporated Jewel Manufacturing Company.

1886 Was elected alderman, Third Ward, Toledo.

1887 Was confined to bed, November. Printed last Nasby letter December 26.

1888 Died February 15, Toledo.

1891 *The Demagogue* was published.

1893 *The Nasby Letters* was published.

Keep thy shop, and thy shop will keep thee.
—*Poor Richard*

Alas! art is long, and life is short! My friends
would comfort me with the idea of a name,
they say, I shall leave behind me, and they
tell me I have lived long enough to nature
and to glory. But what will fame be to an
ephemera who no longer exists? And what
will become of all history in the eighteenth
hour, when the world itself, even the whole
Moulin Joly, shall come to its end, and be
buried in universal ruin?
—BENJAMIN FRANKLIN, "The Ephemera"

Petroleum V. Nasby

CHAPTER 1

Rags to Riches

IN ONE OF HIS FIRST EDITORIALS, David Ross Locke wrote: "We once knew an old Friend who had but one piece of advice to young beginners: it was, 'If they'll only begin right, all will go well. . . .' Franklin is a familiar illustration of what a man can do who begins right. If he had been too proud to eat rolls in the street when he was a poor boy, he never would have been Minister Plenipotentiary to the Court of France."[1] Locke's own beginnings were not auspicious, yet with Franklin as a model he became an extremely versatile and prolific writer, a powerful editor and publisher, a millionaire, and—as Petroleum Vesuvius Nasby—a political satirist rivaled only by Franklin himself in American history. Although Locke was not minister plenipotentiary to France, he was offered the mission to Saint Petersburg or to Berlin by President Grant; and President Lincoln was half serious when he offered "to *swap* places with him."

I *Beginnings*

Locke was born in Vestal, Broome County, New York, on September 20, 1833. His father, Nathaniel Reed Locke, had been a common laborer who, eleven years earlier, had become a "Temperance man so that my two little Boys should not [be] mortified with a drunken Father & thank God I have been able to keep the pledge to this day." Hester Ross Locke, David's mother, was a hard-working housewife, to whom Nathaniel could give his half dollar a day "with the assurance that when wanted it would be forth comming."[2] The parents, both of colonial

Anglo-Saxon ancestry, had moved to Vestal in 1832 where
Nathaniel set himself up as a tanner; but, plagued by bad luck
and ill health, he frequently had to move from one country
town to another. After David's birth, the family moved to
Killawog, about ten miles north, and in 1840 to Marathon, just
over the border in Cortland County. Here for five years the
boy received the only formal schooling he ever had in the old
yellow, country schoolhouse.

David was later described by a schoolmate as "a chunk of a
lad with a shock of tow colored hair, barefooted, with his pants
rolled part way up to his knees and dressed in a sheep gray
roundabout suit. How droll he was, too, and full of pranks, often
bringing upon himself punishment for his mirthfulness."[3] But,
uncouth as he was, he was a good student; and, when he went
to work at the age of twelve, he was a conscientious worker.

David's father was a man of firm principle, and David inherited his stubbornness and some of his principles. Like his
father, he was ever concerned with the good of the common
man. Also like his father, he preached temperance all his life,
both on the platform and in his newspaper writings, although
he did not practice what he preached; his death was probably
hastened by his overuse of alcohol. His consistent hatred of
slavery was inherited from his father. His father was a Methodist,
and as a youth David was leader of his Methodist Episcopal
Sunday School class;[4] and, although he became a broad liberal
in religion and seldom attended any church, he showed his
Protestant training by a lifelong distrust of the Roman Catholic
Church and by a love of Protestant hymnody.

As the eighth of eleven children in a none-too-prosperous
family, David left home and began his career in journalism in
1845. The Cortland, New York, *Democrat* for September 16 and
23 of that year contained an advertisement for an apprentice:
"Wanted at this office, a Boy from 16 to 17 years of age, of
good habits, as an apprentice to the Printing Business. Apply
immediately." And, despite his extreme youth and the fact that
he had to stand on a box to reach the type frame, he got the
job. The *Democrat* was a typical county weekly of the period,
a four-page sheet "devoted to politics, general intelligence, and

agriculture" and composed of editorials, stories, political news, advertisements, and clippings from other papers. It had been founded five years previously by the Cortland County Democrats, who were somewhat in the minority. Like all the other small-town papers of the middle-nineteenth century, it depended chiefly on subscriptions for support; and the publisher, Seth Haight, continually found it necessary to remind his readers to pay up.[5]

Locke, a clever apprentice, made the best of his small opportunities. He achieved a truly remarkable education during his five years of service, so that when he was able to start his own paper only a few years later, it was a model of small-town journalism. His education was both practical and general. He became skilled at setting type, arranging layout, and managing everything from circulation to news gathering; and he developed a powerful and idiomatic writing style and the ability to write on almost any topic of current or antiquarian interest. His business ability he did not have to learn; it seemed inherent.

In 1850, Locke arranged with the Sons of Temperance of Corning, Painted Post, Elmira, West Addison, and other communities in southwestern New York to publish a temperance paper with a guarantee to him of $750 a year, to be raised through fifteen hundred subscriptions. He intended to increase the number of subscribers, and for this purpose gave lectures on temperance through the region. The guarantors did not fulfill their promise however. "I have found," wrote Locke to his brother and sister in Cortland, "that Divisions of Sons of Temperance can break their word as often as other people." He soon sold the subscription list and good will to the *Cayuga Chief,* a temperance paper at Auburn, New York. "As it is," he commented sagaciously, "I come out of it clear. Just got paid for my labor & time. Had I gone on with it, under the circumstances, I should have lost."[6]

As a printer, Locke did not lack opportunities for employment. The number of small newspapers in the United States in the 1840's, 50's, and 60's was astounding. But the pay was poor. The publisher himself, who was also usually the editor, was lucky to make a meager living from his exertions. David Ross Locke was bound to rise, and he did not long remain a mere typesetter. In 1851 he was engaged as a reporter on the Pittsburgh *Chronicle,* and before long he was an assistant editor.[7] On the *Chronicle* he met another young newspaperman, James G. Robinson, who became a staunch friend and after whom Locke later named his first son. When a printer's strike threw them out of work, Robinson and Locke pooled their resources, and with forty-two dollars founded the *Advertiser* in Plymouth, Ohio.

II *Country Editor*

Plymouth was a thriving farm village in north-central Ohio, with a high degree of literacy; but, although at least one newspaper had been attempted there, none had succeeded. "When first we broached the idea [of] establishing a newspaper in this town," Locke wrote a few years later, "it was ridiculed by one half of the community, and received very coldly by the remainder."[8] Nevertheless, the young men set out boldly. The opening address, under the masthead on the second page of the first number, October 22, 1853, expressed their determination and typified the aims that Locke was to express in numerous other newspapers during his career:

SALUTATORY

TO THE FRIENDS AND PATRONS OF THE

PLYMOUTH ADVERTISER:—

In the face of many obstacles in arranging the office, we herewith present our readers [?] with the first number of the *Plymouth Advertiser,* and in doing so, make our politest bow for the favors they have shown us, asking them to excuse the natural vanity of feeling proud of our *first bantling.*

That a town of the size of Plymouth, possessing the business advantages it does, and the extensive trade it already has, and surrounded as it is by an intelligent and reading community, should have been so long without a newspaper, is a matter of no little astonishment to us. True, an attempt was once made, but the failure certainly was not brought about from want of encouragement on the part of the people. We shall make another attempt, feeling perfectly confident that a good paper can and will be sustained, especially as we are determined not only to make it *useful*, but actually *necessary*, resting assured that by sparing no efforts to make our sheet a vehicle of local, as well as foreign interest, people will patronize it. *Nil desperandum* is our motto; if we cannot *command* success, we shall do our best to *deserve* it.

It must be at once evident to any one acquainted with the wants of the people here, that a paper is much needed. The statistics of our post-office will show that there are but few, if any towns of the same size in the State, to which more reading matter is sent, than to ours. But in this day of progression, people are not satisfied with importing their intelligence from abroad; they wish to have papers in their immediate neighborhood, which will keep them informed of what transpires in their own section of country. Until within a short time, and we regret it is still too lamentably common, country newspapers were compendiums—and poor ones too, at that—of city journals, apparently thinking it worth their while to pay little or no attention to what occurred in their locality; and to this cause, probably, more than any other, may be ascribed the insignificant circulation and influence of the country press generally, and the corresponding increase of country subscribers to city papers. In this matter we shall endeavor to introduce an improvement, making our paper as local in its character, as will comport with its general usefulness.

Our object will be to make the *Advertiser* suitable to all readers, consequently it will not espouse the cause of any party. We can do this quite conscientiously, as the purity and incorruptibility of the present political parties may very well be disputed. Time and experience have demonstrated that the *principal* difference, as well as the difference in *principle*, between them, is the "five loaves and two fishes," and the strife is, who shall get them. Were it not for spoils, the "dear people" would not be bored annually with *patriotic* appeals, from *disinterested* office-hunters, to come forward and save this "glorious Republic," before it is irredeemably ruined by *Whigisms*, or *Locofoco misrule*. We are opposed to all demagoguism, and it is high time that every true lover of his country should shut down on those who practise it. But whilst we eschew party politics, so do we despise *neutrality*. We prefer to pursue a middle course, and therefore purpose that the *Advertiser* shall be an *independent* sheet. Having minds of our own, we are determined to speak them fearlessly and candidly, on all topics which may be of importance to our readers, without being trammeled by party ties, or awed by favor. This is an age of progress, and we shall allow ourselves the expansive platform of speaking on political subjects, just what we conscientiously believe to be right and proper.

To the Literary Department of the *Advertiser*, we shall pay particular attention. Its columns will be enriched weekly, with selections of prose and poetry from the best sources we may be able to command. To this feature of our paper, we commend the especial attention of our Lady readers, assuring them that nothing of the least immoral tendency shall ever be found in its pages.

For the Farmer, we shall devote a portion of our paper to the subject of Agriculture, and such other subjects as may be of interest to him. The day is past when "book farming" is sneered at; agriculture is becoming a subject of scientific investigation—farmers who wish to keep up with the progress of the day—those who are disposed to improve on what their fathers did—will be forced to inform themselves of everything which may pertain to their profession. Such, we think, will derive material benefit from what we publish on the subject. We shall also give correct reports of the markets, in this and other places, and endeavor to make them as reliable as possible.

But while paying due attention to the above departments, we shall by no means neglect the general reader. With the aid of the Telegraph, and the speedy transmission of intelligence by railroad, we expect to furnish our readers with the very latest current news of the day, and as there is, at present, every appearance of stirring times in Europe, we will give such a compendium of foreign news, as will keep the readers of the *Advertiser* well posted up in everything of importance which may transpire across the Atlantic.

In conclusion, dear reader, permit us to express our sincerest thanks for the encouragement you have given us. The many favors we have received from you, emboldens us to ask that you will make a few more efforts in our behalf. The more patronage we receive, the better the paper we shall be able to give you. Situated as we are, of course we can have no hope of political "pap;" our enterprise is entirely dependent on our individual efforts, and the favors of those of our friends who may feel interested in the success of our paper. So far, we have received a very flattering subscription list, but it will still require a considerable increase to put the *Advertiser* on a firm basis. We hope those who have held back their names until the first number should be published, will come forward at once, and subscribe, assuring them that they are running no risk whatever, *as the paper is bound to go ahead.*

Respectfully,

J. G. Robinson,

D. R. Locke,

Editors and Publishers Plymouth Advertiser.

The language of Locke's editorials is sometimes overblown and redundant, but not so in comparison to that of his contemporaries in journalism. At its best it shows the refreshing vigor of grass-roots American English; and a cavalier attitude toward polite verb forms and other niceties of school-book grammar only reinforces this quality. At barely twenty, Locke had developed a style that showed little change throughout his voluble career.

The two boys did remarkably well in living up to their salutatory promises. The first issue of the *Advertiser* was typical of what was to follow. The first page contained the literary matter: a sentimental poem "The Stars," a comic poem by E. B. Slater, a fine Simon Suggs story, and an uplifting editorial. The second page contained editorial matter and local and foreign news; the third, miscellaneous news and business news; and the fourth, the agricultural column with articles on sheep, glue, hog raising, and grapes. Of the forty-two columns in all, fewer than seven columns were filled with advertising, but the financial success of the enterprise was attested by the rapid increase in advertising during the first months of the paper.

After the first issue, much of the writing in the paper was borrowed from other journals—except for the editorials and some of the literature. In the first issue the editors apologized for the lack of "exchanges," but that was soon remedied. The system of exchange was a journalistic institution of the day; it was customary for editors to send free subscriptions to other editors throughout the country with the understanding that they would get a free subscription in return. Material was freely copied from one paper to another; and, if it was especially good, it might be reprinted repeatedly through the nation. It was thus that Artemus Ward, Mark Twain, and Petroleum V. Nasby won national fame.

Politically, Locke soon showed himself to be a Democrat, although his abhorrence of the spoils system and his stubborn free will kept him—then and always afterward—independent of political patronage. When his refusal to "espouse the cause of any party" was attacked by the Pittsburgh *Post*, he replied in an editorial of November 5: "There is a heap of satisfaction in Treasury plunder, as the Post must certainly have experienced by this time, as its hand has been in Uncle Sam's pocket two-thirds of the time it has existed. Spoils have well-nigh ruined the Whig party, and will kill the Democratic, unless it purges itself of the leeches that are sucking its life blood." His political acumen demonstrated itself early. In January, 1854, he denounced Stephen A. Douglas' effort to nullify the Missouri Compromise of 1820: "The friends of freedom must be on their guard, and not permit the clap-trap that the introduction of slavery into Nebraska is 'impractical' to direct them from making every effort to prevent the spread of this foul blot on the otherwise fair escutcheon of our country."[9] He favored the idea of "annexation in general" and recommended that the United States forcibly annex Lower California, Cuba, the Lobos Islands, the Sandwich Islands, and Mexico. On women's rights and temperance, he placed himself with the reformers.[10] Indeed, he already held the major political and social opinions that he was to fight for throughout his life, and he anticipated much of the platform of the Republican Party before it existed.

Working together as reporter, editor, publisher, circulation manager, and advertising solicitor, Robinson and Locke established a newspaper which has lasted to this day. And, in addition, they operated a successful job-printing business. They perhaps did not work so hard as they pretended, for it is related that

Locke, stealing a leaf from Franklin's autobiography, often left a lamp burning late in the office to make it appear that he was working while he went out and enjoyed himself for the evening. The partners also found time to take part in the initiation of an Agricultural and Mechanical Society for the holding of fairs in Plymouth and in a movement for the construction of a plank road.[11] Nevertheless, they were boasting of the number of their subscribers and advertisers as early as November 19, 1853; in January of 1854 they sported a new and more pretentious title block; and by the time they left the *Advertiser* on October 6, 1855, they could claim that the job work and advertising alone would reach sixteen hundred dollars a year.

While in Plymouth, Locke also found time to court Martha Hannah Bodine, daughter of a respected citizen. The marriage, which took place on March 7, 1855, was a solid and lasting one. Martha was a faithful and diligent housewife and a pleasant and loving mother to the three boys that were born to them. Although she apparently contributed little to Locke's thought, she gave him a home life that he had not known since the age of twelve. It is likely that Locke's sentimental poem "Hannah Jane" (1882) was a sort of acknowledgment of the self-effacing devotion that his wife gave him. "For me she rubbed herself quite out," he wrote; "The most unselfish of all wives to the selfishest of men." Though Locke was not a selfish man, it is probable that his ambition drove him to devote less time to his family than he would have liked. More than once Martha was left to care for the family while David was trying to establish himself in a new position in another town. There is no evidence that she ever complained of the meager income that the country editor brought home or of his precarious financial undertakings in the 1870's that eventually brought him considerable wealth.

His unceasing lifelong labor was motivated in part by a desire to give his sons a better start than he had had. In 1864 when Robinson Locke was eight, his father wrote him a letter of advice and admonition from Bellefontaine, Ohio, where he had gone to work on the Bellefontaine *Republican*: "I think about you a hundred times a day, and it troubles me a great deal that

I cannot be with you. But so it is. I must work, work, work to earn money to educate you and Eddy, and to clothe and feed you, and your good ma she works and works and works to make your clothes and cook your food. Why do we do this? Because we love you."[12]

Locke's relentless drive amounted to an obsession. In one of his last letters, written in 1887, he wrote: "I have tried to live so as to have no regrets. I hate them."[13] Yet he did have regrets: regrets not only for what he considered the neglect of his family but also for an addiction to drink that he barely managed to bring under partial control somewhat late in his life. "For twenty years," he said, "I never went to bed one single night truly and duly sober." But he claimed to have quit drinking "at once & totally & forever" in 1883, although oral report has it that his claim was not strictly true.[14] Much of his writing can be explained as a kind of expiation. His continual hammering away on the subjects of women's rights and prohibition is symptomatic of the depths of his feeling of guilt. He was able to characterize Petroleum V. Nasby unforgettably because Nasby was his creator's alter ego. Both the author and his creation were vulgar, combative, whiskey-drinking fellows, inclined to stockiness and to red noses. Nasby was what David Ross Locke might have been had he not possessed a gnawing conscience.

Locke's ambition drove him in 1855 to move to Mansfield, Ohio, where he became one of the publishers of the *Herald,* an established weekly in a town somewhat larger than Plymouth. He took with him his wife, as well as his partner Robinson and the latter's new wife. The partners pooled what capital they had accumulated and joined with Roeliff Brinkerhoff, a Mansfield lawyer who had been editing the paper during the illness of the retiring editor. The partners, Brinkerhoff & Co., began the publication of the Mansfield *Herald* on September 12, 1855, although Locke did not actually leave the Plymouth *Advertiser* until about a month later. According to Brinkerhoff's reminiscences, Robinson, who was "steady as a clock," managed the job and printing departments; Brinkerhoff did the political writing; and Locke wrote the local news and contributed the necessary spice. A series of three letters signed "Sniggs" was among

Locke's first experiments in comic writing. One of these letters
told about a cow, given to Sniggs by his mother-in-law as a
wedding present, that had an incurable habit of wandering back
to its original home. Sniggs discovered that he was not the only
son-in-law to have received it as a gift, only to find it impossible to keep. The letters were said to have contained so much
true autobiographical material that the Bodine family raised
objections and that Locke destroyed the columns that were on
file in the newspaper office.[15]

It was in Mansfield that Locke became an avowed spokesman
of the Republican Party. Brinkerhoff wrote in the partners'
salutatory: "Politically the *Herald* will be *Republican,* out and
out. We shall oppose to the full extent of our ability, the further
extension of the area of human bondage."[16] For Locke, the
switch to the anti-slavery party was not really a switch at all.
His political feelings already represented those of a growing
number of Midwesterners who formed, under various banners,
the Republican Party in 1854. Ohio in particular was an early
proving ground of Republican principles. It produced such men
as Salmon P. Chase, an abolitionist and later Lincoln's Secretary
of the Treasury, and Joseph Medill, editor of the Cleveland
Leader and one of the founders of the Republican Party. On
the other hand, it produced Clement C. Vallandigham, outspoken Southern sympathizer who was banished from Union
territory by Lincoln's administration, and Samuel Medary,
editor of the Columbus *Crisis,* the only newspaper in the North
that consistently used the term "nigger" after the Civil War
had begun. In the Ohio of the late 1850's, it was almost impossible not to take sides, and Locke chose early and emphatically.
Nor did he stray from the cause throughout the remainder of
his life.

Locke had already demonstrated an ability to make a financial
success of a newspaper, but he was apparently not so successful
at holding on to his money. According to Brinkerhoff, he was "a
little wild and rather fast," and was unable to pay his share of
the partnership. Robinson and Brinkerhoff became the sole
owners on January 24, 1856. "Circumstances, over which we
have no control," wrote Robinson in the February 6 *Herald,*

"sometimes renders it necessary for friends, old and tried friends, to part." A few weeks later Locke was in Bucyrus, Ohio, where he managed to produce enough capital or credit to become publisher and editor of the Bucyrus *Journal* on March 20. On April 17, 1856, Locke's brother joined him as co-proprietor of the *Journal*, and on April 11, 1857, James G. Robinson replaced the brother and again became Locke's partner, remaining as publisher and editor after Locke departed in 1861.

The Bucyrus paper, under the editorship of J. A. Crever, had been a Republican organ in a Democratic county, and was admittedly a commercial failure. Locke's family had been increased by the birth of his first son, Robinson, just five days before he took over the *Journal*. Because of his financial needs, he advertised that he would exchange subscriptions for "wood, lumber, beef, pork, turkies, chickens, butter, eggs, potatoes, flour and MONEY."[17] But by dint of hard pounding on Republican principles and by colorful abuse of the Democrats, he made the paper a success and boasted as early as September 13 of his first year that "The Journal has the Largest Circulation of any paper in Crawford County."

Locke's salutatory in the Bucyrus *Journal* was borrowed almost word for word from Brinkerhoff's Mansfield statement. The paper was to be "REPUBLICAN out and out," but Locke significantly omitted Brinkerhoff's pledge to "avoid personalities, slang, and everything that tends to irritate uselessly." Instead, he began a vociferous feud with the Democratic Bucyrus *Forum*. On March 18, 1858, for example, he replied to the personal abuse of the *Forum* editor:

> The Editor of the *Forum* finds fault with our legs. We acknowledge ESTILL excells us in that particular. He has a marvelously symmetrical pair of trotters, and *nothing else*. When he was formed, the architect commenced at the feet and built upwards. After he had the legs finished, he knocked off for dinner, and alas! never thot of the job again—forgot it entirely. Having nothing else to boast of, we can easily excuse his intense admiration of those members. If he keeps on in his present course, the people of Bucyrus will be much relieved in about six months by seeing him *travel* on them.

The rival editor did not depart in six months; in fact, he remained to continue the abuse of David Ross Locke and his successor after Locke's departure. But the amount of factional feeling stirred up in Crawford County was demonstrated in September, 1861, when a crowd of partisan rioters damaged the *Forum* office.[18]

The *Journal* was a forthright political organ, but it also contained a good deal of popular literature, both borrowed and original. Since the borrowing was not always acknowledged and since the original material was never signed, it is seldom possible to determine authorship with much certainty. We may hope that the sentimental verse was not by Locke, but he did write a great many stories, mostly in a romantic vein. "The Journeyman's Secret" (July 24, 1856) was about a taciturn and miserly printer, who, it turned out, was saving his money to pay for an operation to restore the lost eyesight of his sister. "The Border Heroine" (January 1, 1858) was a tale of an Arkansas housewife who defended her household against bandits. "Story of a Woman's Slipper" (November 1, 1860) was a sentimental love story. And perhaps the best of Locke's fiction in the *Journal* was "The Bow-Legged Knight" (October 29, 1858), a short burlesque of romantic fiction that the author later revised to fit the dialect of Petroleum V. Nasby and reprinted in *Divers Views, Opinions, and Prophecies of Petroleum V. Nasby* (1866).

In Bucyrus, Locke became involved in helping the escape of runaway slaves, and he carried on a crusade against the Knights of the Golden Circle, the organization devoted to obstructing the prosecution of the war. "Treason!" he wrote on October 4, 1861. "There is enough of it in Crawford county to keep the hangman busy a month." He was examined before a grand jury for his allegations against the Knights in what Robinson considered an attempt by the Democratic majority to embarrass him.[19]

The Civil War having begun, Locke volunteered for service; and on November 5, 1861, he received a commission as second lieutenant in the Sixty-Fifth Regiment of the Ohio Volunteer Infantry, with the proviso that he recruit thirty men to form a company for that regiment within fifteen days. On November

16, the young editor's valedictory appeared in the *Journal:*
"There are other duties to perform—our imperilled country needs
the services of her every son, and without a sigh at the sacrifice,
I go to aid in the work of her salvation, esteeming those the
unfortunate who are obliged to stay at home." But he never
went to war. According to one highly questionable story, the
governor refused the commission on the grounds that Locke
was more valuable as a journalist than as a soldier.[20] Another
possible explanation is that his drinking made him unacceptable.
Perhaps the most likely surmise is that he was unable to
raise his thirty men and the commission was revoked. The
editorials and the advertisements soliciting volunteers in the
Journal of that period show without doubt that it was difficult
to gather recruits in Crawford County. It is said that Locke sent
a substitute into the army, a story that would not conflict with
any of the explanations of his non-participation.

Locke was still in Bucyrus as late as November 23, probably
trying to collect subscription payments due him.[21] By December
13, however, he had become owner of the Findlay, Ohio,
Hancock Jeffersonian, which he began editing on December 27.
This new paper was more of a family newspaper than the
Journal had been. "Politically the paper will continue to represent
the Republican sentiment of Hancock County," Locke wrote in
the December 27 issue. "Politics, however, shall not occupy
more than its fair share of space. . . . In short, I shall do all in
my power to make the *Jeffersonian* a live newspaper." Under
Locke's predecessor the *Jeffersonian* had been more dead than
alive. A humdrum weekly of news, editorials, exchanges, and
advertisements, it was lacking in variety, local interest, and
format, and was written in the stiff "journalese" of the day. In
his closing editorials, the retiring editor, S. A. Spear, complained
of lack of support by the Union (Republican) men of Hancock
County; and he warned that Locke would need their subscriptions as much as he had.

Locke set about to enliven the paper and to increase its
circulation and advertising. He soon gave over the first page,
which had been devoted to cut-and-dried news reports, to

fiction, poetry, human interest stories, and inspirational essays. The January 17, 1862, issue, for example, contained "The Crab Apples: A New Farce in One Short Act"; "Animal Content," an essay on cats; "Youth and Manhood," observations on coming of age; "Forward Not Backward," comments on growing up; "The Sick in Bed," an article on practical nursing by Florence Nightingale; "Women and Auctions," an article by Mrs. M. C. Ames; and several short items on such matters as a saying of Professor Louis Agassiz and the report of the escape of a nun from a French convent. There was still room on the front page for "Congressional" news. The signed articles were, of course, from other newspapers. The second page contained news and Locke's outspoken editorials, while the third was devoted to local and miscellaneous items. As were all of his previous newspapers, the *Jeffersonian* was a four-page sheet, and the fourth page was soon devoted almost entirely to advertising, although there was some advertising also on other pages. The paper soon showed signs of thriving; in fact, it was on the *Jeffersonian* that Locke achieved fame, although he probably realized but little profit.

The outstanding attraction of the Findlay newspaper was the Nasby letters. Locke wrote the first one, "Letter from a Straight Democrat," for the April 25, 1862, issue, and followed it immediately with "Another Letter from Petroleum V. Nasby" in the May 2 issue. He henceforth continued the letters in approximately every second issue, although he never achieved any predictable regularity. The early letters were of more local interest than the later, more famous, ones. Findlay and Hancock County were specifically named, as were many local citizens; and county and state politics received as much attention as national. It is the letters from the *Hancock Jeffersonian* that Lincoln read in pamphlet form, and the President is said to have admired them more than any other writing of his time. In appreciation of Locke's genius, he offered the writer "any place you ask for—that you are capable of filling and fit to fill." Locke did not accept the invitation, but he did use his influence to secure the President's pardon for an Ohio deserter. And many years later, in 1885, Locke expressed the reverence he had come to feel for Lincoln in an article in the *North American Review*.[22]

By 1865, Locke's pamphlet, *The Nasby Papers*, was printed in London as well as in Indianapolis; his first book, *Divers Views, Opinions, and Prophecies of Petroleum V. Nasby*, was in preparation; and the Nasby letters themselves were being reprinted from the *Jeffersonian* in newspapers all over the country. The editor evidently became dissatisfied with his prospects in Findlay and left there February 10. Leaving his family in Findlay, he worked for a while on the Bellefontaine, Ohio, *Republican* until he accepted in October the position of editor of the Toledo, Ohio, *Blade*.[23]

III   Man of the World

With the removal of the country editor to the established city newspaper, Locke had arrived, at the age of thirty-two, at a position of trust and security that he had never before known. The *Blade*, founded in 1856, came under the sole proprietorship of Alonzo D. Pelton in August, 1865; and Pelton's business acumen prompted him to hire Locke at a salary of two thousand dollars a year, a substantial sum in that day.[24] There were a daily, tri-weekly, and weekly *Blade*, although the tri-weekly and weekly were but condensed versions of the daily and were aimed at a purely local circulation in the immediate vicinity of Toledo. The paper had stood staunchly for the Union and the administration during the Civil War,[25] and it enjoyed the patronage of the Republican majority of Lucas County.

But Locke was far from satisfied with the status quo. Though he wrote no salutatory, he was provoked by the rival Toledo *Commercial* into stating his political position in the February 1, 1866, issue: "We state positively and unequivocally, that the BLADE is not the organ of any body. It is not controlled by any clique or faction. . . . Under the new management as under the old, the BLADE will speak its mind on all subjects of interest to the people, freely, fearlessly and independently." Remaining independent of political patronage, Locke's position was nonetheless firmly Republican. But he was concerned with making his paper something more than a political sheet. In one of his earliest issues, October 17, 1865, he apologized for the amount of space taken up by politics and explained that he could offer more variety when he became better acquainted with Toledo and its people. As with his earlier papers, his success lay in the breadth of his appeal. The *Blade* soon contained— besides foreign, national, and local news—vigorous editorials on political and social issues; popular literature; essays; a great variety of clippings from other papers; and special columns by commissioned writers, as well as the Nasby letters.

Locke's formula, along with the appeal of his hard-hitting journalistic style, was immediately successful. By February 1, 1866, he was able to state: "our circulation is more than double that of any paper in Northwestern Ohio, and increasing with a rapidity unparallelled in the history of newspapers in this part of the heritage." At the end of his first year, Locke's salary was doubled. In 1867 he became a partner in A. D. Pelton & Co., owners of the *Blade*. In 1873 he helped organize the Blade Printing & Paper Co., of which he became the president in 1874. In 1876 he was owner and president of the Toledo Blade Company. From 1865 to his death in 1888, he held a dominant position in the paper, though his active participation varied according to the demands of his health and the many outside interests with which he was concerned. In 1884 he asserted that he had sold the *Blade* four or five times but had always had to take it back within two years because of the drop in circulation that inevitably occurred.[26]

It was the *Weekly Blade* that drew Locke's most devoted attention and that reached truly national importance. He dubbed it "Nasby's paper," for he was already better known by the name of his fictitious creation than by his own name, and he featured the Nasby letters in the weekly. Besides containing selected material from the daily *Blade*, "Nasby's paper" was aimed at the farm family and emphasized agricultural and market news and features and many items of particular interest to women. Locke's ideals were explained in a promotional pamphlet issued by the Toledo Blade Company in 1885:

His idea of a weekly paper was one which should contain, each week, matter of interest to every member of the average family. It should contain a news department so all-embracing and perfect that when the reader was through with it he or she would have a perfect knowledge of what the world had done during the week, this accompanied with editorial comments making clear to the mind of the reader the philosophy of the events, a department for women and girls especially, which would not only be entertaining but instructive, the best literature for the entertainment and elevation of the taste of the people, regular articles on agricultural and mechanical industries, the markets, the politics, and the social movements of the day, and opinion, forcibly put, on all topics of interest, and above all the advocacy of everything calculated to make men and women better.[27]

The pamphlet declared that the *Weekly Blade* had the "largest circulation of any weekly family newspaper in the United States." There is no doubt that it was read in virtually every state in the union, and the circulation figures showed that it had risen from about one thousand copies a week in 1865 to two hundred thousand in 1884. Its political influence was incalculable, and it provided a window on the world for many a farm family.

The David Ross Locke of the late 1860's was not very impressive to look at, except for his bursting energy. The best description of him is one by Mark Twain, who had lately befriended him on the lecture circuit:

Nasby is about thirty-five years old. He is compact, solid, heavy. He weighs a hundred and seventy or eighty, perhaps. There is nothing of a dainty look about him, but on the contrary, he is as burly and vigorous as a theatrical blacksmith. His energy is invincible. After traveling all day and lecturing every night for months together, he was as fresh as ever. His attire is unfashionable, but he cares nothing for that. It does not fit, but that does not concern him. He is not graceful on the stage, but that does not distress him. He is not as handsome as I am, but more picturesque.[28]

Locke's manner was positive and gruff, though he could be heavily playful. It is related that he liked to sing hymns at the top of his powerful lungs while going about his newspaper work. His drinking was probably at its worst at this time. He later asserted that he frequently lectured when he was so drunk that the audience was invisible. The prim George Washington Cable, who reported that statement in a private letter, called him "a coarse man of the harder world, successful and unsatisfied," and summed up his description: "He's a bad dream."[29]

Locke's lectures were among his most successful ventures. He began in 1867 at about the same time that James Redpath was organizing his famous Boston Lyceum Bureau. Though Artemus Ward and others had been successful lecturers with the aid of private managers, Redpath saw the potentialities of a national agency that would take care of publicity, correspondence, scheduling, and rate fixing for the benefit of both the lecturer and the organization that hired him. The Redpath agency immediately became the center of what by this time was a big business, for the popular lecture was one of the favorite forms of entertainment—and sometimes instruction—in the United States. The most famous lecturers of the age were Redpath clients: John B. Gough, the prohibitionist; Anna E. Dickinson, the feminist; Thomas Nast, the cartoonist; and Josh Billings and Mark Twain, the humorists. "Nasby," as he was billed, was in the top rank. He demanded and received a minimum of two hundred dollars a performance—a sum that Mark Twain asked in 1871 but probably did not receive—and, by lecturing six nights a week for nine or ten months, he made what he claimed to be the longest and most lucrative lecture tour ever recorded, netting over $30,000 in one season.[30] He delivered the same lecture hundreds of times until it had been heard in nearly every town in the country. He was often classed with Ward, Billings, and Twain; but his lectures had little in common with theirs. While they were content with a few words of wisdom interspersed with a good deal of entertainment, Locke always had a timely message and drove it home with his usual sledge-hammer force. It is ironic that, while the chief complaint against Twain and Ward was their lack of seriousness, Nasby's audiences were sometimes offended that he gave them political argument when they expected mere entertainment. "I wonder what on earth they did expect Nasby to talk about?" remarked Twain. "Poetry, no doubt."[31]

As Locke's position in journalism became secure, his other interests—literary and financial—multiplied amazingly. He wrote at least seven pamphlets over the signature of Petroleum V. Nasby—some composed of previously written newspaper letters, others newly written, and all designed to influence specific political events. In addition to *The Nasby Papers* (1864), there were *Androo Johnson, His Life* (1866), *The Impendin Crisis uv the Democracy* (1868), *Inflation at the Cross Roads* (1875), *The President's Policy* (1877), *The Democratic John Bunyan* (1880), and *The Diary of an Office Seeker* (1881). It is a matter of speculation as to how much influence the pamphlets had, either on the course of American political history or on the fame of Petroleum V. Nasby. At any rate, they brought the works of Nasby within the price range of the most indigent reader.

Besides the pamphlets, Locke was the author of ten books: five volumes—with considerable overlapping—of collected Nasby letters; the mock-oriental tales *The Morals of Abou Ben Adhem;* the long poem *Hannah Jane;* and the novels *A Paper City* and *The Demagogue.* These were in addition to uncounted stories and poems never collected in book form.

Locke published many of his works himself under the names of the Toledo Blade Company; Locke & Jones, Publishers; and Locke Publishing Company. And he also published works of other writers. In 1878 he persuaded John McElroy to write a series of articles on his experiences in Southern prisons during the Civil War. Published in the *Weekly Blade,* the articles were received with such "exceeding favor" that Locke published them the following year under the title of *Andersonville.* The book was one of the great first-hand documents of the Civil War, and as such it was republished in 1957. "We only desire," wrote McElroy in his Preface, "that the Nation shall recognize and remember the grand fidelity of our dead comrades, and take abundant care that they shall not have died in vain."

Another of Locke's publishing schemes was less successful than the exposé of Southern prisons. In December, 1872, he launched *Locke's National Monthly*. Subtitled "A Magazine of American & Foreign Literature," it was a genteel literary periodical for readers who were not quite up to the *Atlantic*. "We cannot claim for the NATIONAL MONTHLY a successful competition with the larger and higher priced Magazines of the day," went one editorial comment. "But we are earnestly and honestly committed to the building up of a publication which shall meet the universal demand for instructive and entertaining general and family reading, at the lowest possible cost."[32] Made up of forty-eight, two-column pages per issue on coarse paper, the magazine contained original poetry, fiction, and timely essays by lesser-known authors and reprintings from other magazines of writings of better-known authors. Political controversy was avoided, and there was a pervading moral tone both in the contributions and in the "Notes and Comments" of the editor. Locke's own contributions were the most noteworthy of the original material; he later published most of them as *The Morals of Abou Ben Adhem* (1875). The magazine was published for more than three years, but the scarcity of copies today suggests that it never had a large circulation.

In the midst of editing, publishing, writing, and lecturing, Locke took on the additional job of a New York City newspaper, the *Evening Mail*. Information on this aspect of his life is scant. It is certain that he retained his interest in the *Blade* and continued contributing to it, but meanwhile he was connected with the *Mail* between 1871 and 1879. On February 1, 1871, the *Mail* moved its offices and Robert Johnston became sole publisher. It was probably Johnston that engaged Locke, but the name of the editor was never printed. In 1878 Locke was listed as "Publisher and Treasurer" on the letterhead of the *Mail's* stationery, and he signed himself as "Manager."[33]

Locke apparently attempted to handle the New York daily on somewhat the same lines that he had used so successfully to manage small-town weeklies, yet maintaining the polite and high-minded tone that the *Mail* had already established. It was regularly a four-page paper—though more pages were often added—with eight columns of fine print per page. Meant to appeal to the genteel metropolitan family, it contained matter by special correspondents; regular articles on fashion, amusements, art, books, and recent magazines; educational news; women's news and special articles for women; and national and international news and editorials. An announcement regularly printed under the masthead at the time Locke joined the paper described it as follows:

> THE EVENING MAIL is now the Largest, Sprightliest, and best two-cent evening paper published in New York; Contains all the Cable, Financial, and Telegraph News, and has the Largest Circulation of any evening paper among the influential classes of the community.
>
> This paper commends itself to Advertisers, inasmuch as it is thoroughly read in the home circle of its patrons.

But on October 24, 1871, that announcement was replaced by another, which probably reflected Locke's concern with reform:

> It is a thoroughly Independent Organ of the honest men of both political parties who hate official corruption; who desire the adoption of some scheme of Civil Service Reform; who want the National taxes so adjusted and reduced as to impose the fewest possible burdens on industry and commerce; who are opposed to railroad and other monopolies; who are opposed to unnecessary legislation by the Federal Government; who are in favor of Temperance Reform; who are interested in educational, charitable and religious movements, and generally, of those who believe that the increasing evils of our times demand fearless, non-partisan newspapers, which will sustain the cause of Truth, Honesty, and Practical Christianity on all occasions and under all circumstances.

Locke's motives in joining the *Evening Mail* were probably more than financial. His growing concern with corruption in government was evident in the *Blade* editorials as well as those in the *Mail*. For Locke, the center of political corruption was New York, and here he could continue the battle waged so well by his friend Thomas Nast, the cartoonist of *Harper's*

Weekly. Nast and "Nasby" had once considered going on a joint, illustrated lecture tour, and their long-considered plans for a joint book were at this time culminating in the publication (1872) of *The Struggles of Petroleum V. Nasby* with Nast illustrations.[34] Through his violent cartoons in *Harper's*, Nast had succeeded in bringing public concern to the point of destroying the Tweed Ring that had dominated Tammany Hall and New York politics for years. But Tammany corruption continued and, according to Locke, vitiated the entire Democratic Party. "The great reform of this generation," said a *Blade* editorial of July 8, 1872, "is the destruction of the corrupt Democratic organization." Furthermore, the Democrats had endorsed Horace Greeley, Liberal Republican nominee for the presidency, to oppose the regular Republican, Ulysses S. Grant, in the 1872 campaign; and many Republicans were switching their allegiance. Greeley was editor of the powerful New York *Tribune,* and Locke—ever loyal to Grant—may have hoped to use his influence in opposing Greeley through the *Evening Mail.*

But, unfortunately, the *Mail* was not Locke's proper vehicle. In the Nasby letters, which continued in the *Blade,* he delivered telling blows at Democratic corruption, but the Nasby letters did not appear in the *Mail.* The carefully non-partisan policy and the gentlemanly tone of the *Mail* so effectively tied Locke's hands that the paper turned out to be but another New York newspaper. Its political influence was insignificant. The paper continued to exist for many years, but it was never one of the great New York journals.

Meanwhile, Locke's business interests must have demanded much of his time. He was an active partner in the Bates & Locke advertising agency in New York and Toledo in the early 1870's. He was investing heavily in real estate in Toledo, and he took a vigorous part in community development there. He was a trustee of the Northwestern Ohio Medical College, founded in Toledo in 1882; he was one of the promoters in 1886 of the unsuccessful Citizen's Natural Gas Company, which was to have supplied the City of Toledo; and at the time of his death he was a director of the Northern National Bank of Toledo. He promoted the work of G. W. N. Yost in improving the typewriter, and he was one of the earliest users of this machine. In 1884 he incorporated the Jewel Manufacturing Company to make Blade sewing machines, which were sold with subscriptions to the Toledo *Weekly Blade.* Although he sustained some losses, his estate was worth a quarter of a million dollars in the 1870's, and he is said to have died a millionaire. In a bantering mood, he once told Mark Twain: "I'll tell you, Clemens.... I've settled down upon the belief that there is but one thing in this world better than a dollar, and that's a dollar-and-a-half."[35]

In 1870, Locke became interested in Free Religion, as preached by Francis Ellingwood Abbot of Toledo, and he privately contributed three thousand dollars a year for three years to the publication of *The Index,* a Toledo periodical that Abbot founded "to increase pure and genuine RELIGION in the world ... to destroy every species of spiritual slavery, to expose every form of superstition, to encourage independence of thought and action in all matters that concern belief, character or conduct."[36]

In 1876 and 1879, Locke ventured into the drama. *Inflation, or The Xs of the X Roads,* "an original comedy-drama in 5 acts," by D. R. Locke and Charles Gayler, was produced early in 1876 but with no apparent success. There was no doubt of the success of *Widow Bedott,* or *A Hunt for a Husband,* which Locke composed from *The Widow Bedott Papers* of Frances M. Whitcher, that had been extremely popular in the magazines of the 1840's and had been published in book form in 1855 and 1864. The widow, a garrulous and pretentious old gossip, was portrayed by Neil Burgess, because no actress would take the part. Performed in Providence, Rhode Island, on March 28, 1879, "it was a success from the moment Burgess appeared."[37] Brought to Haverly's Lyceum Theatre in New York on March 15, 1880, it ran seven weeks. It made the name of Burgess, who devoted the rest of his career to female impersonations. The actor continued to perform it on into the 1890's, and late in his life cut it down to a one-act to be used in vaudeville. At least two other companies performed it in the 1880's, with Charles B. Bishop and Joseph Palmer playing the widow. George Clinton Odell calls the play "another typical thing of the '80s, a long-enduring joy to rural communities and not unpleasing to larger centres."[38]

In the 1880's, Locke was able to delegate more and more of his business. His son Robinson, who had begun as a reporter on the *Blade* at the age of seventeen, was gradually taking his father's place on the paper. Locke had reached a secure middle age, and in 1881 he took time for a vacation in Europe, making capital of it however by writing the *Nasby in Exile* papers for the *Weekly Blade* and later publishing them as a book. After a lifetime spent in avoiding political office for the sake of independence, Locke changed his mind in 1886 and launched himself into grass-roots politics, beginning at the bottom. Despite the pessimism of his friends, he ran successfully for alderman of the Third Ward in Toledo. But he had scarcely a year of active politics. In November, 1887, he was confined to bed, with what was diagnosed as consumption. His phenomenal health had finally broken under the years of hard work and equally hard drinking, and vacation trips had not helped. He wrote the last Petroleum V. Nasby letter in December, 1887. He died at home February 15, 1888.

David Ross Locke was greatly mourned. The daily *Blade* printed obituaries and memorial tributes through the February 21 issue. The weekly devoted most of its February 23 issue to the event and featured the remaining poetry and fiction of Locke during the ensuing half year. The tribute of Ex-President Rutherford B. Hayes may be cited as typical of the genuine admiration that was expressed:

I am at this moment in receipt of the announcement of the death of D. R. Locke. I beg you to convey to his family my sincere sympathy with them in their bereavement. With his pen Mr. Locke gained for himself a conspicuous and honorable place among those who fought the good fight in the critical years of the anti-slavery conflict before the war. During the war and after it, he was surpassed by no writer in the extent and value of his influence on the march of events until its great results were substantially secured. He had the satisfaction of receiving from Mr. Lincoln himself the first meed of praise for his matchless services in the hour of his country's trial.[39]

CHAPTER 2

Of Slaves and Presidents

I F THERE IS AN AMERICAN who reads these pages," Locke wrote in *Nasby in Exile*, "and does not from this time out, make politics as much a part of his business as planting his crops, that American does not know what is good for him. Government is the most important matter on this earth."[1] Locke's own concern with government was lifelong. It grew from his early training and experience. His father's feelings about slavery and intemperance, his own innate sympathy for the underdog, and his education in journalism—all created a more-than-ordinary social consciousness. The mental jump from social consciousness to political action was as natural for him as it is for us today. That society could and should be organized by government; that poverty, disease, and crime were not only the results, in part, of bad government but that they could be alleviated by good government; that the material welfare of the common man was the responsibility of government—these Locke took for granted from the beginning while his contemporaries toyed with *laissez faire* and "the less government the better." He believed in government of the people, by the people, and for the people. He foresaw, however dimly, the welfare state.

Though usually on the side of the reformer, Locke was no mere visionary. He took no part in the communistic and utopian schemes that were rampant. His constructions were always practical, and his only tools were the ballot and the press. His life was devoted to the slow process of public enlightenment and to the long fight for truly universal suffrage. He frequently grew impatient with delay, and he constantly deplored political dealings that obstructed progress; but he never wavered from his faith in democratic processes. And he rejected all forms of authoritarianism, whether in the Roman Catholic Church, the slave-holding South, the monarchies of England and the Continent, or the reform movements that would force their benefits on an unwilling public.

I *Republicanism*

Born in the year that Andrew Jackson began his second term as President, Locke was originally a Democrat. His political principles comprised most of the things popularly associated with Jacksonianism: "equality against privilege, liberty against domination; honest work against idle exploit; natural dignity against factitious superiority; patriotic conservatism against alien innovation; progress against dead precedent."[2] To these causes he remained loyal, though he was one of the earliest and most lasting converts to the Republican Party. Jibed by a rival editor for switching parties, he replied in 1856:

Why, Locke, a couple of years ago, you was a ranting, raving Democrat—*Forum.*

Barrin' the "ranting and raving," the above is true. We left that party when it ignored the Democracy of Jefferson and Jackson, and resolved itself into an association for the purpose of slavery extension, and if the editor of the Forum had had in his composition one spark of political honesty he would have done as we did, refused to eat his own words, and deny the soundness of doctrines he had maintained for years. When you find us playing second fiddle to any party-leaders, changing as their interest compels them to change, and dancing as they pipe, just let us know. We have not changed, we stand where we always did, and claim yet to be a Democrat—a national Democrat—not one of the Douglas patent, whose principles were manufactured to order some two years ago—but one of the kind who believe that "all men were created free and equal." This is our creed, the political god we worship, and always has been.—When the bogus-Democracy knocked it off its pedestal and set up that great sham, squatter sovereignty, in its place, we refused to render homage, and every day we are more convinced that we did right. We are still a Democrat, and an extremely zealous member of the only really Democratic party in existence.[3]

The issue of slavery made Locke a Republican; he did not particularly sympathize with the Eastern industrialists who were an important segment of the party. Nor was he a hot-headed abolitionist of the William Lloyd Garrison or Harriet Beecher Stowe kind. His Republicanism was fierce but not extreme. The cause of equality was a moving force in his life, but he recognized that it was not to be won overnight. Until after the Civil War had begun, he did not advocate the abolishment of slavery but resisted its extension into new territories: "Allowing none of [the abolitionists] to exceed us in *hatred* (we mean that word) of slavery, we held, and therein differed with them, that where slavery existed we had nothing whatever to do with it, and could not lawfully reach it if we wished to."[4]

It was on this ground that he became an admirer of Abraham Lincoln as early as 1858. In a November 12 editorial of that year, he pointed out Lincoln's popular majority in the Illinois senatorial election and the "unreal victory" of Stephen A. Douglas and his principle of popular sovereignty.[5] Lincoln's firm opposition to that doctrine won Locke's strong support in the presidential campaign of 1860.

The threatened secession of South Carolina drew forth one of Locke's best satirical editorials in the Bucyrus *Journal*, a *tour de force* that was later rewritten to make the first Nasby letter in *Divers Views, Opinions, and Prophecies of Petroleum V. Nasby*. The satire was double: it mocked the presumption of South Carolina, and it ridiculed the Southern sympathizers in little Crawford County, of which Bucyrus was the seat, and which had voted for Douglas:

> Secession is the order of the day, and as soon as South Carolina goes out of the Union, ripping up the Confederacy, there will be an admirable opportunity to redress grievances. Crawford County will at once secede from Ohio, establish a Government of her own, and proudly take her place among the

nations of the earth. We have too long submitted to the imperious dictates of a tyrannical government, and gladly will our chivalrous high-minded, high-toned, hi-falutin citizens seize this glorious opportunity of rending the chains from their limbs, hurling them in the face of their foes, and renouncing all allegiance to a government they hate, and a people they despise. . . . [6]

In the disheartening year of 1861, Locke came as close as he ever did to renouncing a Republican administration (not counting Andrew Johnson's). On October 25, he belabored the administration for indecision. On November 1, he complained of the lack of a good Union general, though he did not directly blame Lincoln. On November 8, he questioned the wisdom of Lincoln's removal of General John C. Frémont, and he later called it an "inexcusable blunder." On January 3, 1862, he demanded more military action: "We have men enough to do it, arms enough, munitions enough, and we have enough of everything." And, on February 14, he violently attacked the extravagance of a ball given by "Mrs. Honest-Old-Abe."[7]

However, with the beginning of the Nasby letters in April, his attitude began to change. There was no questioning of the administration in the letters. Like many others, Locke favored using those Negroes that could be freed to support the Union forces; and, as it appeared that Lincoln was moving toward a policy of emancipation, Locke became less critical of him. On September 26, 1862, in "The President's Proclamation," he endorsed the emancipation plan, and he never dispraised Lincoln again. In the election campaign of 1864, he backed Lincoln as "the honest and faithful defender of our rights and liberties against the wanton attacks of the rebellion." Lincoln's only fault, Locke continued, was "that he has not hung as many damnable traitors North and South, as the Constitution and the voice of the people would have warranted him in doing."[8]

But the Emancipation Proclamation did not end Locke's efforts for Negro equality. He demanded equal suffrage, legal rights, and opportunities in labor and education. With the assassination of Lincoln and the end of the War, he looked to Andrew Johnson to carry forward Lincoln's firm but moderate policy toward Reconstruction. Early in 1866 he defended Johnson's moderation against his extreme Northern critics: "Such men [as Wendell Phillips] do some good in acting as pioneers in reforms, but it would be a mercy if, when they reached a certain point, they could be deprived of speech."[9] But Locke was eventually though reluctantly disillusioned. Johnson's veto of the Civil Rights Bill in March and his proclamation declaring the war at an end in April brought forth Locke's guarded disapproval. Finally Locke's wrath was ignited when Johnson's followers met with the Copperheads at the Philadelphia Convention in July to attempt to defeat the anti-Johnson Republicans in Congress.

It had been well for Johnson if he had heeded the many editorial warnings of the Toledo journalist. Locke's renown was now established, and both as editor of the *Blade* and as author of the Nasby letters, he wielded influence. In the ensuing months, he went all out against the President. In addition to his widely reprinted writings in the *Blade,* he published two Nasby pamphlets and two hard-bound books before 1869, when Johnson's administration was ended. All of them were aimed at Johnson and his Democratic confreres. The pamphlet *Androo Johnson, His Life, Includin' His Infancy, His Boyhood, and His Dimocrisy and Abolitionism, Separate and Mixed,* published in anticipation of the Congressional elections of 1866, concluded with Nasby's full endorsement—and thus Locke's condemnation—of Johnson:

> Ez these pages is goin to press I hev to announce that I take back all I sed about ablishnism at all in the subjick uv the foregoin sketch. He's gone back on em AND IS OURN! I HEV RECEIVED MY COMMISSION EZ POSTMASTER—the guillotine is workin by steem, and the appointees is all Democrats uv the genooine stamp. Backed up by them eminent patriots, Doolittle, Seward, Beecher and Cowan he's all rite. The writer hereof hez faith ez large as a Postmaster's commission. He's a greater nor Jaxan, purer than Washington. My pen is hentzforth A. Johnson's, the Patriot of Tennessee!

Androo Johnson was released under at least three other titles by different publishers: *Andy's Trip to the West, Swinging Round the Circle,* and *Nasby's Life of Andy Jonsun.* In the same year of 1866, Locke published *Swingin' Round the Cirkle,* a book made up of Nasby letters from the *Blade.* Both the pamphlet and the book made political capital of Johnson's trip to the tomb of Stephen A. Douglas. Ostensibly a pilgrimage to Chicago to honor the late hero of the moderate Democrats, Johnson's journey was actually a campaign to gain popular support for the moderates as opposed to the radical Republicans in Congress. Accompanying him were General Grant and Admiral Farragut, who were received with acclaim, while the President's appeal was unsuccessful. Nasby was supposedly appointed chaplain of the President's party, and the title of the book, "Swingin' Round the Cirkle," was quoted from Johnson's speech, which he repeated time after time with little change, not realizing that telegraphy made it possible for his audience to read what he had said before he arrived. A sample of Nasby's log of the journey will illustrate:

UTICA.—The President spoke here with greater warmth, and jerked more originality than I hed before observed. He introdoost here the remark that he didn't come to make a speech; that he wuz goin to shed a tear over the tomb uv Douglas; that, in swingin around the circle, he hed fought traitors on all sides uv it, but that he felt safe. He shood leave the Constooshn in their hands, and ef a martyr wuz wanted, he wuz ready to die with neetness and dispatch.

ROME.—Here we hed a splendid recepshun, and I never heard His Majesty speek more felicitously. He menshuned to the audience that he hed swung around the Southern side uv the cirkle, and wuz now swingin around the Northern side uv it, and that he wuz fightin traitors on all sides. He left the Constitooshun in their hands, and bid em good bye. I received at this pint only 130 petitions for the post office, wich I took ez a bad omen for the comin election.

LOCKPORT.—The President is improvin wonderfully. He rises with the occasion. At this pint he mentioned that he wuz sot on savin the country wich hed honored him. Ez for himself, his ambishn wuz more than satisfied. He hed bin Alderman, Member uv the Legislacher, Congressman, Senator, Military Governor, Vice-President, and President. He hed swung around the entire circle uv offises, and all he wanted now wuz to heal the wounds uv the nashen. He felt safe in leavin the Constooshn in their hands. Ez he swung around the circle—

At this pint I interrupted him. I told him that he hed swung around the cirkle wunst in this town, and ez yooseful ez the phrase wuz, it might spile by too much yoose.[10]

Following *Swingin' Round the Cirkle* came *Ekkoes from Kentucky,* Locke's third book, which brought the Nasby letters up through the November elections of 1867, and continued to pound away at Johnson. Finally, *The Impendin Crisis uv the Democracy,* 1868, was a pamphlet designed to promote the election of Ulysses S. Grant against Democrat Horatio Seymour. Just how much this barrage of propaganda affected the impeachment proceedings against Johnson, the embarrassment of the Democratic Party, and the success of Grant's campaign is impossible to say. At any rate, Grant felt it important enough to offer Locke the political spoils of a select foreign mission.

Meanwhile, Locke was pursuing the cause of racial equality in his lecture. His most comprehensive statement of his position on the Negro problem was in "Cussid Be Canaan," delivered in 1867 and 1868. He did not directly attack Johnson in the lecture; he accused those elements in both parties who were willing to relinquish the ideal of human equality. Whether or not the Negro was generally equal to the white in natural endowments, Locke believed that the right of every man to the opportunity to prove himself should never be abridged:

I would not make them superior to the white. I would do nothing more for them than I would for other men. But I would not prevent them from doing for themselves. I would tear down all bars to their advancement. I would let them make of themselves all that they may. In a republic there should be no avenue to honor or well-doing closed to any man. If they outstrip me in the race, it proves them to be more worthy, and they are clearly entitled to the advantages resulting. There is no reason for this inequality. Knowing how deep the prejudice is against the race, knowing how low down in our very natures its roots have struck, I demand, in our renewed and purified republic, the abrogation of all laws discriminating against them. I demand for them full equality with us before the law. Come what may, let it lead to what it will, this demand I make. I make it as a worshipper of true Democracy; as one who believes in the divine right of man—not white man, red man, or black man, but MAN, to self-government. I make it as one who will be free himself; and that he may be free himself, would have all others free. I demand it, not as a gracious gift to the colored man of something we might, if expedient, withhold, not as a right he has earned by service done, but humbly, and with shame in my face at the wrong we have done, I would give it him as returning a right that was always his, a right to which he has a patent from God Almighty; a right that we had taken from him by brute force, and the taking of which by us was almost the unpardonable sin. I demand it, for until it is done our boasted freedom is a sham, and our pretence of republicanism a miserable lie. I demand it, for I would have no privileged classes in this government, for fear that some day my children may by force be deprived of the rights I enjoy by a class arrogating to themselves superiority. I demand it, because I believe governments were instituted on earth for the protection of the weak against the strong, and that in a republic the ballot is the weak man's only protection. I demand it, because we cannot afford to give the lie to our professions; because we cannot afford to say to the world one thing and do another.[11]

David Ross Locke was one of the best friends the American Negro has had. Not only was he forceful but practical and reasonable. He triumphed in the ratification of the Fifteenth Amendment in 1870, but his message is just as valid in the 1960's as it was in the 1860's.

In the 1870's and 1880's, Locke remained suspicious of the Solid South and could at times be accused of waving the bloody shirt. His publication of John McElroy's *Andersonville* in 1879 kept sectional bitterness before the public despite the author's apology in his Preface: "For the great mass of Southern people we have only the kindliest feeling. We but hate a vicious social system, the lingering shadow of a darker age, to which they yield, and which, by elevating bad men to power, has proved their own and their country's bane." And an editorial in 1880 in the *Blade* expressed Locke's feeling that the friendship prof-

[51]

fered by many Northerners was not truly reciprocated by the South: "The era of conciliation and good feeling seems to be like the fun in a practical joke: there is never enough of it to go clear around."[12] Although the Negro question ceased to be the great divisive element that it had been in the 1860's Locke kept a vigilant eye on the South and on the Democratic Party. He was quick to point out abridgments of civil rights; and, through the Nasby papers as well as his editorials, he continually exposed and satirized the unreconstructed Southerner. His violent pen was not adapted to conciliation, even when conciliation was his party's cry. Today he serves to remind Americans that democracy's goal of human equality is yet to be fully achieved.

II *Corruption in Government*

With the election of Grant and the Constitutional guarantee of Negro suffrage, Locke's primary interest shifted to other things. The big issue during Grant's two terms was political corruption and the spoils system. Both parties had their scandals. In answer to the Crédit Mobilier scandal of 1873, the Republicans could point to the Tweed Ring, which was destroyed in 1871 but which had left a lasting stain on Tammany Hall politics. Locke remained loyal to Grant and to the regular Republican Party, even when a number of prominent Republicans defected to the "Liberal" cause and nominated Horace Greeley for the presidency in 1872, with the support of the Democrats.

Locke's position on political corruption had already been stated, and he invariably associated it with the practice of giving away political appointments as rewards for party services. Nasby is the perfect embodiment of the corrupt office seeker. In one of the earliest Nasby letters, he gave his qualifications for political office:

> 1st. I want an offis
> 2d. I need a offis
> 3d. A offis wood suit me; ther4,
> 4th. I shood like to hev a offis.
> I maik no boasts uv what my speshel clames air, but I hev dun the party sum servis.[13]

And Locke clearly advocated reform in 1870, when he said: "The only way to restore purity to our legislative bodies is to take away, so far as possible, all appointing power from both the legislative and executive departments of the government."[14]

But, during the 1870's, Locke was handicapped by the recurrent exposés of favoritism, conspiracy, and fraud within the Grant administration. Although both political parties proclaimed a policy of reform, it was more difficult for the party in power to overlook its own blemishes. Speaking for the party in power, Locke's writing lacked the effectiveness that it had shown in the 1860's, when party issues were more distinct. For a while—from December, 1869, to December, 1870—he moved Nasby to the Sixth Ward in New York City, where the late Postmaster of Confedrit X Roads became the proprietor of the Harp uv Erin S'loon. As a rallying point for the Irish Democrats of the ward, the saloon and its patrons symbolized the vote buying and ballot-box stuffing that were notorious in New York. But, as Locke became busier, his writing became less consequential. The Nasby letters suffered—even in quantity.

It was not until Samuel J. Tilden ran against Rutherford B. Hayes in 1876 that Locke again found a proper target. Though Tilden's principal argument was reform—he had been instrumental in breaking up the Tweed Ring—there was evidence that he was not above vote buying, while Hayes seemed as clean as the driven snow. Locke's attack on Tilden was as ruthless as that on Andrew Johnson. And it did not end with Tilden's bitterly contested defeat, for there was still danger that he would run again in 1880. In the pamphlet *The President's Policy*, Locke wrote in the guise of Nasby:

> Why repeet the histry uv that campane? When it wuz nessary to hev another vote, so anxshus wuz he for purity, he offered thousands for one Oregon elector, and didn't he offer to buy up Looisiana entire, and didn't he threaten war and blood ruther than not hev the Goverment to purify? Finally the infamus high jint, wich he hisself appinted, went back onto him, and declared the yooserper Hayes the President. Then broke a noble heart! The most tetchin meetin I ever saw wuz

that uv the great reformers, Tilden, John Morrisey, Oakey Hall, Fernandy and Ben Wood, and the principal leeders uv Tammany when the nooze uv the Hayes triumph reeched em.[15]

The danger of political power was a lifelong theme for Locke. For himself, he carefully avoided political office until, in his later life, he could be free of all appearance of personal interest. Nasby, on the other hand, was concerned with politics only as a matter of personal interest. A major target in the lecture "In Search of the Man of Sin" (1870) was political corruption. And *The Demagogue* (1891), his most serious novel, exposed the machinations of political power.

Locke was quite aware that neither political party was blameless. Although he was generally concerned with exposing the Democrats, the conscienceless protagonist of *The Demagogue* was a Republican. Like Hugh Henry Brackenridge, his predecessor in political satire, Locke recognized the peculiar susceptibilities of democracy—the dangers of demagoguery, machine politics, balloting frauds, and graft. He did not blame democracy itself, but called for broader suffrage along with broader enlightenment as the remedy.

III *Political Economy*

Sympathizing as he did with the poor and downtrodden, Locke was no blind follower of the moneyed interests in the Republican Party. He generally supported the economic program of the party, but not usually with the enthusiasm that he showed on other issues. He approved the protective tariff and opposed the free trade "heresy," but he believed that "capital, rather than labor, should bear the chief [tax] burdens of the government."[16] He encouraged the expansion of railroads and urged the people of Toledo to vote for taxes to aid them, but he attacked the railroads' monopolistic tendencies and favored federal restrictions on them.[17] In his next-to-last Nasby letter Locke concurred with the *Blade's* policy and came out firmly for the protective tariff, which was under attack by Grover

Cleveland's Democratic administration. But even here, his sympathies lay with the American laborer, who he claimed was the beneficiary of the duty on foreign imports.

Nasby's support of Cleveland's position revealed Locke's real opposition to it: "I know his eggslency is rite, for every paper in England approves uv his message. Ef ther wuz ez much yoonanimity this side uv the water in approvin his vews that ther is on tother, it wood be clean sailin. In consekence uv the barrin out uv English goods from Ameriky, the English operatives and capitalists hev bin sufferin fer yeers. In the interest uv broad hoomanity we want to transfer that sufferin to Ameriky."[18]

On the issue of paper money Locke was more fervent. The Republicans, with the support of the business and financial interests of the East, were generally for sound money; but the farmers of the West wanted a more or less unlimited issuance of paper money. The extreme inflationists organized the National Greenback Party in 1875, and Locke devoted six Nasby letters to the subject. In these letters, later issued as *Inflation at the Crossroads*, Nasby became a financier:

> The Corners hev red the speeches uv Honest Ole Bill Allen and that other gileless patriot, General Samyooel Cary, uv Ohio, ez well ez the Pennsylvany platform, on the momenchus subjick uv More Money, till they hev ben worked up to a state uv absloot madnis. The Corners are jist the same ez all other impecoonius people—they want More Money, and the idee uv Honest Bill Allen, that, to git it, all yoo hed to do wuz to ishoo it, filled our idees uv finanse eggsackly. It's simple and ezily understood.
>
> I determined to put the idee into practice, and to that end sejested to my friends the organizashen uv a Bank uv ishoo, under the name and title uv "The Onlimited Trust and Confidence Company uv Confedrit X Roads."
>
> I hed some trouble to git the citizens into it, but I finely succeeded. I explained to the people that more money wood be an advantage to the debtor class, wich, ez nine-tenths uv em is in debt to Bascom, the grosery keeper, settled em. They hailed with joy any movement that wood wipe out their scores and give em new credit at his bar.

To Bascom, and them ez I intended to hev in the management, I showed that more money meant increased trade, and ez the money woodent cost anything but the printin we coodent lose anything. . . . [19]

Nasby's scheme worked well for a short time; but, when the citizens discovered that their money would not buy anything outside the Corners, they became an infuriated mob: "No gentle gazelle that I ever heerd uv," said Nasby, "ever skimmed the plain ez I did. I did not cease runnin till I got into the middle uv the big swamp."

Locke's economic views were simple and conservative: sound money and the protection of labor and capital at home. Above all, he believed in the dignity and necessity of hard work. His own struggle from "rags to riches" gave him some understanding of both labor and capital, and he wanted America to be a land of opportunity for all as it had been for him.

IV *Women's Rights*

A subject of permanent interest to Locke was feminism. Probably remembering the plight of his own hard-working and unrewarded mother, he ever deplored the social restrictions that kept women from achieving what they might. His remedy, as usual, was political—woman suffrage. His interest in improving the conditions of women showed itself as early as 1854 in the Plymouth *Advertiser,* "A Family Newspaper," which featured material for the entertainment and edification of women. "Women's Rights," an editorial in the April 8 issue, showed his sympathy with the feminist movement. At the time of his death, the *Weekly Blade*—also advertised as a family newspaper and featuring Emily S. Bouton as Literary and Household Editor—was publishing a series of sermons by the Reverend Thomas DeWitt Talmage on women's "powers and privileges." Throughout his editorial career Locke published numerous articles on women's rights. In 1872, for example, he applauded the successful attempt of two women to vote in Toledo.[20] Although women played only a minor part in the Nasby letters, there were women's crusades against Bascom's saloon in letters of 1874, 1883, and 1884. Locke's poem *Hannah Jane* (1882) was a tribute to a woman's silent martyrdom and an indirect plea for better conditions.

His most effective statement of his views was in the lecture "The Struggles of a Conservative with the Woman Question" (1868). He was not fanatical; he would not want women less feminine but would give them freedom to develop their abilities: "I would give the ballot to woman for her own sake, for I would enlarge the borders of her mind.... I would put on [women's] shoulders responsibilities that would make rational beings of [them]." Not only for women's sake did he plead but for the sake of humanity. "I would strengthen her, and through her the race." Furthermore, he argued, true "Republicanism" demanded universal suffrage. "I would give the daughters of the poor, as I have helped to give the sons of the poor, the power in their hands to right their own wrongs." Locke did not live to see the passage of the Nineteenth Amendment, but he contributed to its passage as he had to that of the Fifteenth amendment.

V *The Irish*

David Ross Locke was sometimes wrong, but he never got too old or too inflexible to change his views, notwithstanding his lifelong consistency on race, women, and temperance. This fact is evidenced by his almost complete reversal of opinion toward the Irish. His earlier view amounted to strong prejudice against them. As usual, his main reason was political. The great wave of Irish immigration was at its height during his lifetime. During the 1860's, 1870's, and 1880's, well over a million and a half residents of the United States were of Irish birth. A large proportion of these lived in New York City, where their poverty and ignorance were eagerly exploited by the machine politicians of Tammany Hall. Locke caricatured the Irish mercilessly in the Nasby letters, particularly the series of December 10, 1869, through December 12, 1870, where Nasby became a saloonkeeper in New York. Nasby described the formal opening of his saloon:

It resulted ez I anticipatid. At first we hed speeches, and toasts. Mr. O'Rafferty replied to the toast, "Our adoptid country." He sed the term "Our adoptid country" wuz a happy one, for so far ez Noo York waz conserned the sons of Erin hed adoptid it. He hed bin charged with a lack uv love for this country. He repelled the charge with scorn. Why shoodn't he love this country? In wat other country wuz votes worth a dollar apeece? Where else cood sich a man ez he hev so high a posishen ez Alderman, and only two years on the ground?

Mr. O'Toole jined in the sentiment. Where else under the canopy cood a man like hisself who coodent read be a skool director? He hed often bin thankful that he turned his face toward Ameriky the minit his time wuz out in the prison at Liverpool. Ther wuz less risk in holdin offis in Noo York, than in burglary in England, and the results wuz shoorer.

Ther wuzn't much more speech-makin. The drinkin went on fast and furious tho, and ez I antissipated, before the twenty gallons wuz eggsausted I wuz very drunk, and incapable uv any effort, mental or physikle, and the others were in very much the same predicament.[21]

Another reason for Locke's asperity toward the Irish was his distrust of their religion, which probably antedated his animosity toward them. Though generally an exponent of religious tolerance, he felt that the authoritarianism of the Roman Catholic Church was incompatible with freedom of thought and hence with intelligent voting. He feared the authority of the priest as he did that of the party boss. "Republicanism and Catholicism can never flourish together," he wrote in 1853; "...when they are brought in contact, one or the other must fall."[22] Yet even his attitude toward the church softened when he observed the self-sacrifice of Irish priests in their efforts to help their suffering people in Ireland.

Still another reason for Locke's anti-Irish sentiment was the fear that completely unrestricted immigration would encourage the worse elements of foreign lands to seek shelter in America. "We Do Not Want Them," a *Blade* editorial of July 5, 1880, stated: "If the truth was known, it would show that the majority of all who have entered into the riots of the past in our large

cities are foreigners of the lowest class, of whom their own
people were only too glad to be rid." Despite Locke's concern
for the poor and oppressed, and despite his faith in the land of
opportunity, he looked with suspicion on the admission of
"paupers and criminals" who, he feared, would damage American institutions.

Throughout Locke's residence in New York in the 1870's, he
remained anti-Irish; and, when he went to Europe in the
spring of 1881, one of his first public observations was that of
fraud in the solicitation of funds for the Irish Republican movement. His conversion is attributed to James Redpath, the lecture
manager, in 1881, although as early as December 24, 1880, a
Blade editorial on Christian brotherhood had said: "Ireland's
heart is throbbing in burning agony at her wrongs." According
to Locke, Redpath guaranteed to convince him of the incredible
suffering of the Irish under English landlordism by taking him
to the Irish villages where tourists seldom ventured. From
Cork, they went to Fermoy, about fifty miles to the north, and
on to the village of Mitchelstown, on the edge of the Galty
Mountains. Here and in the surrounding country, they saw
poverty and futility that made an indelible impression. Observations in other parts of Ireland corroborated the impression, and
Locke became one of the most outspoken advocates of Irish
home rule. Indeed, it was reported that he spoke out so loudly
while in England that the British government ordered his arrest
but that his departure prevented the carrying out of the order.

His new impression of the people of Ireland illustrates his
changed attitude: "There is no man in the world, not excepting
the Frenchman, who will work longer or harder than the Irish-
man. There is no race of men who are better merchants or more
enterprising dealers, and there is no reason, but one, why Cork
should not be one of the largest and richest cities of the world.
That reason is, English ownership of Irish soil."[23] Locke devoted
several chapters of *Nasby in Exile* (1882) to the Irish; and, in
the pages of the Toledo *Blade* and in public addresses, he
attempted to make up for his earlier bias and to promote the
cause of Irish independence.

VI *Temperance*

Locke's longest crusade was against alcohol. The son of a temperance man, he was editor of a temperance paper at seventeen, and some of his last writings were about the evils of alcohol. His motives were both personal and political. His own case gave him experience with the evils of excessive drinking and the tenacity of the alcohol habit. An article in the *Weekly Blade* for March 5, 1886, entitled "The Confessions of a Drunkard" was probably partly autobiographical, and he openly confessed his difficulties in breaking the habit to Mark Twain and G. W. Cable. Apparently Locke preached temperance and finally prohibition from the firsthand conviction that alcohol made slaves of its victims. Prohibition, he thought, would save future generations from servitude. And he may even have felt that it might save him.

Locke also attacked alcohol from political motives. Nasby, of course, was a rousing example of the general effects of liquor in politics. Nasby would commit any fraud or treachery for drink, and he also knew how to use it to attract others of his kind to his own political ends. The "storekeeper" Bascom was the real power in the Confedrit X Roads because, through the sale of liquor, he had mortgages on the lands and the souls of the citizenry. Knowing this, Nasby tried to keep on the good side of Bascom and to gain his support in political manipulations. In a fit of honesty, Bascom once explained the source of his power:

"Wat a happy life yoors is, Bascom!" sed Kernel McPelter.

"Happy!" remarkt Issaker Gavitt, "I shood say so. Nuthin to do but to sell likker at a profit uv 200 per cent, and every customer you git ded shoor for life."

"Gentlemen," sed Bascom, onbendin, for he wuz drinkin hot whisky, too, "there is advantages in runnin a wet grosery, but it hez its drorbax. It is troo that ther is 200 per cent profit, or wood be ef you got paid for it. But, alas! yoo don't git paid for it all. A ingenuous youth comes into my bar, wich hez a small farm, and he gits to takin his sustenance. That wood be all rite for me ef he cood only take his sustenance and take keer uv his farm at the same time. But he don't, and whenever the necessity uv takin sustenance begins to be regler, just when he mite be uv the most yoose to me, I hev notist ther wuz alluz a fallin off in his corn crap. Corn won't grow onless yoo plant it, hoe and tend it, and a man wich becomes a regler customer uv mine don't plant, tend nor hoe to advantage.

"Then, not hevin corn to sell, he can't pay for likker, and ez he must hev it, he goes on tick, and finelly mortgages his place. Troo, I alluz git the place, but it wood do better for me ef he cood keep on workin it, spendin the proceeds at my bar. Ther is very few men wich kin do this.

"And then death is another drawback to my biznis. Ef a man cood only drink regler and live to be 70, it wood be suthin wuth while. But they don't do it. They are cut off by the crooel hand uv death jist when they git to be yooseful to me. This one goes uv liver disease, tother one uv kidney trubble, rhoomatism sets in and knocks one uv em off his pins, softenin uv the brane kills another——"

Joe Bigler, who jist dropped in, doubted the last disease. "No man which hed a brane to soften wood tetch the d——d stuff," sed he. . . .

This wuz the longest speech I ever knowd Bascom to make. Wat he sed is troo. I hev eggsperienced it in my own person. . . .

I shel keep on, I spose, forever, but despite wat Bascom sez ez to the dror-box I shood like to be in his place.[24]

The power of the saloonkeepers to get votes by persuasion, free drinks, bribery, or threats was vastly enhanced, according to Locke, when they were organized by the importers, distillers, and brewers and began to operate on higher political levels than the local. The subject became all absorbing to Locke during the Ohio election campaign of 1883. The Republican legislature of 1882 had passed a law taxing liquor dealers two hundred dollars a year. The brewers and distillers, Locke alleged, assessed each saloonkeeper and raised the largest sum of money ever expended in an Ohio election up to that time. With it they openly contributed to the Democratic victory that put G. R. Hoadley in the gubernatorial chair and a Democratic majority in the legislature. Not only that, but when the legislature procrastinated, the brewers managed to get a majority in the state supreme court to declare the tax law unconstitutional. Locke's attack began during the campaign and continued to his death. In editorial after editorial, in both the daily and weekly *Blade*, he reiterated the slogan "Pulverize the Rum Power":

> What we want to impress upon our readers, is the fact that beer and whisky is a power, which, as parties are divided and are likely to be, holds the balance of power in all the states, controlling not only the legislative and executive branches of the state governments, but the judicial. They control the political actions of the thousands of saloon-keepers, whom they own, body, soul, boots and breeches; they have millions of dollars and the most lucrative business in the world at stake, and they are utterly and entirely without interest in matters political except as it effects their peculiar traffic.
>
> Ohio stands before the world as a state whose executive, legislative and judicial departments are the mere instruments of the liquor interest, under a bargain to carry out its behests.
>
> ... In brief, the time has come to do something toward destroying this monster which aims at the control of the country.
>
> The BLADE has already outlined the only way to *Pulverize the Rum Power*.[25]

The only solution, Locke came to feel, was absolute prohibition, and he emphatically endorsed every measure that would lead to that end. In December, 1883, he went to Maine to investigate the success of prohibition, which had been in effect there since 1846. Frankly recognizing the existence of bootlegging, he examined—with apparent relish—the illegal sale of liquor and the effects of the law on the economic, political, and moral welfare of the state. His account, published in the *Weekly Blade* for December 20 and 27, was no mere objective report. Having started with the predisposition to prove his point, he let nothing stop him. The results of this investigation and of others he conducted in Toledo and elsewhere, Locke published in an article in the October, 1886, issue of the *North American Review*. In it he stated his last views on the subject with thoroughness. He asserted that "No man can touch it [alcohol] without fastening upon himself a craving for more"; and he recognized, as some twentieth-century pathologists have asserted, that alcoholism "is a disease, not a vice." "Rum," he said, "is the direct source of 90 per cent. of all the crime and pauperism of the country," and prohibition reduced crime and pauperism accordingly. Prohibition, then, was the remedy; and it would eventually win out: "In five States, Maine, Iowa, Kansas, Minnesota, and Georgia, Prohibition is an accomplished fact, and the sentiment in favor of it is rapidly spreading."

Locke's prediction was correct, but it took more than thirty years for the prohibition amendment to become part of the Constitution—and it was then virtually unenforceable. Thus Locke was a vigorous champion of the nineteenth-century reforms that led to five amendments to the Constitution—the Thirteenth, Fourteenth, and Fifteenth, dealing with abolition and civil rights; the Eighteenth, prohibition; and the Nineteenth, woman suffrage.

CHAPTER 3

The Reverse Logic of
Petroleum V. Nasby

THE TREMENDOUS POPULARITY of Petroleum V. Nasby
was a symptom of his madding times. Hailed by three
presidents, Lincoln, Grant, and Hayes, Nasby was read no more
fervently by the farmers of Hancock County, Ohio, than by such
proper New Englanders as James Russell Lowell and Charles
Sumner. That Locke's drunken, illiterate Copperhead should be
condoned by the genteel can only be explained by the fact that
he was their scapegoat—exactly what Locke intended him to be.
Nasby was the incarnation of the worst elements of democracy—
the ignorance, greed, and corruption that the genteel usually
refrained from seeing—and he was identified with "the opposition." The opposition was, of course, the Democratic Party;
and all sorts of Republicans, from the radical abolitionists to the
most liberal, were able to release their hatreds upon the sage
of Confedrit X Roads. Nasby's outrageous lies and shocking
vulgarity were only to be expected. There were things in the
Nasby letters that would hardly have been tolerated from
Mark Twain or from Walt Whitman. His praise of public figures
amounted to violent personal abuse. All this was possible
because of the "reverse logic" of Locke's method. Everything
Nasby said was to be spurned. His hopes were the reader's
fears; his arguments demonstrated their own falseness; anything
he endorsed the reader would reject because Nasby had endorsed it.

I *Origins*

Locke hammered out the Nasby letters from the materials of American comic journalism that he found at hand. Crackerbox humor before 1860 found its most congenial outlet in the newspapers, although comic magazines, the almanacs, and the theater were also available. Jack Downing, Sam Slick, and Simon Suggs became famous in the newspapers, and they were imitated or paralleled by many others. With the advent of the penny newspaper in the 1830's, the common American discovered cheap and accessible reading matter; and publishers and editors were quick to cater to the mass audience. Because national and international news was slow in arriving and sometimes difficult to obtain in the days before telegraphy and the national news services, editors relied on local news, editorials, and humor to appeal to their readers. A really original comic writer could make a success almost overnight out of a small newspaper. Especially in the small towns and in the Western cities, people bought newspapers in order to read their favorite comic columnist; and the paper's financial well-being was almost entirely dependent on circulation, for advertising did not pay as it does today.

Among Locke's comic predecessors in journalism, a half dozen stand out as most profoundly influencing Petroleum V. Nasby. Benjamin Franklin may well be called the father of American comic journalism. The influence of his autobiography upon Locke has been suggested, but the low-brow wit of his Poor Richard and the common-sense criticism of society in the letters of Silence Dogood helped spark the whole tradition of American humor. Franklin's hoaxes, too—such as "An Edict by the King of Prussia" and "The Sale of the Hessians"—provided a precedent for the dead-pan delivery of the tall tale, and perhaps directly inspired Locke in the use of comic journalism as a political weapon.

The other five journalists were Seba Smith (Jack Downing), James Russell Lowell (Hosea Biglow), Charles Farrar Browne (Artemus Ward), Johnson J. Hooper (Simon Suggs), and

George Washington Harris (Sut Lovingood). Smith (1792-1868) created the Yankee Jack Downing in the Portland, Maine, *Daily Courier*, in 1830 "to show the ridiculous position of the [Maine] legislature in its true light, and also, by something out of the common track of newspaper writing, to give increased interest and popularity to his little daily paper."[1] Before long the green but cagy Jack was hobnobbing with presidents, and his "letters" were being reprinted widely in newspapers around the country, according to the custom of free exchange of copy among journalists. Smith used the letter form as a vehicle for political satire. The Downing letters were mostly the correspondence that Jack addressed to his friends back home as he toured the Eastern seaboard, but they also included the letters to Jack from some of his friends. Like the Nasby letters, they appeared with no introduction or commentary by the author; the characters spoke for themselves. The authentic rural New England dialect gave a flavor of homespun common sense that appealed to the reading public. And the political views of the author—for the letters always concerned politics—were more effectively communicated than by any amount of straightforward editorial writing. Smith continued writing the Downing letters until 1859, and meanwhile he had many imitators, some of whom were not above posing as the original Jack Downing.

James Russell Lowell (1819-91) deliberately composed *The Biglow Papers* as political propaganda—"thinking the Mexican war, as I think it still, a national crime committed in behoof of Slavery, our common sin, and wishing to put the feeling of those who thought as I did in a way that would tell." The First Series appeared from 1846 to 1848 in the Boston *Courier* and in the Boston *Standard;* the Second Series appeared in the *Atlantic Monthly* during the Civil War. It was Lowell's character Birdofredum Sawin that most directly influenced Nasby. "I meant to embody in him," Lowell wrote, "that half-conscious *un*morality which I had noticed as the recoil in gross natures from a puritanism that still strove to keep in its creed the intense savor which had long gone out of its faith and life." Like Nasby, Sawin was a scapegrace who defected to the South during the Civil War, and some of his escapades seem to have been specifically imitated in the Nasby papers. Lowell, who recognized Locke's indebtedness to him, hailed the newcomer among the ranks of political satirists: "I feel as if I could in some sort claim to be an *emeritus,* and I am sure that political satire will have full justice done it by that genuine and delightful humorist, the Rev. Petroleum V. Nasby."[2]

The creator of Artemus Ward, Charles Farrar Browne (1834-67), was Locke's junior by seven months; but he had already gained national renown before the Nasby letters were thought of. Browne had stumbled upon the idea of the Artemus Ward letters while trying to fill his columns as local editor of the Cleveland, Ohio, *Plain Dealer.* The letters attracted such astounding attention that the author soon made Artemus his mouthpiece for satirical comment on American society. But, though politics was frequently mentioned, the Artemus Ward letters were never primarily political in intent. "I hav no politics. Nary a one," said Artemus, who knew "how to cater for the public."[3] His catering more than verged on rascality, but he was a lovable rascal whose views on reform movements, religious experiments, and popular notions were generally those of his author. Like Jack Downing, Artemus used the letter form without introduction or commentary by the real author; but the form soon became a mere formality by means of which Artemus could relate what had happened to him and express his opinions. Like the Downing letters and *The Biglow Papers,* the Artemus Ward letters were in a New England dialect; but Artemus, who was supposedly from Indiana, represented the common American more than the New Englander. In addition to dialect, Artemus was one of the first to use misspelling for its own sake; such spellings as "hav" and "cum" were not a matter of regional pronunciation but rather eye-dialect for comic effect. With the great American emphasis on correct spelling as the first step toward polite learning, Browne used comic spelling to mock social pretentiousness.

It is reported that Browne suggested the character of Petroleum V. Nasby to Locke. And Locke himself asserted that he had worked with Browne on the Cleveland *Plain Dealer*. There is no proof that Locke ever worked on the *Plain Dealer,* but it is likely that the two met as fellow newspapermen in Ohio, though they spoke for opposite political parties.[4]

Johnson J. Hooper (1815-63) and George W. Harris (1814-69) represented the humor of the old Southwest, which also contributed to the creation of Nasby. Locke knew the work of these writers, for he had reprinted their stories in the Plymouth *Advertiser* and in the *Hancock Jeffersonian.* Both Hooper's Simon Suggs and Harris' Sut Lovingood were amoral rogues who boasted of their roguery. Suggs's motto was, "It is good to be shifty in a new country," and Lovingood turned the tables on any would-be critic of his morals by citing in his Preface, "Evil be to him that evil thinks." The authors of both were more interested in a good story than in its moral implications, and the trickery and violence of some of the stories amounted to sadism. With Nasby, Locke went a step further and sustained the Northern penchant for a moral by making Nasby an object lesson in immorality. The deviltry and violence of the Southern humorists were turned against them in a sense, for the characters in the Nasby letters represented the worst in Southern character. Locke was not the yarn spinner that Harris and Hooper and their fellow Southern humorists were, and there was more talk and less action in the Nasby letters than in their yarns. Yet Locke relied on plot—the narrow scrape, the quick turn of events, the rude fall from dignity—to add interest to the letters more frequently than did Browne or Lowell or the other Yankee wits. In his use of language, Nasby was also more closely akin to Simon and Sut than to Artemus or even Birdofredum Sawin. Rather than the highly quotable sayings of the latter, Nasby was more inclined to roll on and on, reveling in exaggeration and sometimes in sordid detail. The Nasby dialect was neither Yankee nor Southern, although Southern dialect was imitated in the speech of Nasby's Kentucky friends.

Foreshadowings of Nasby can be seen in Locke's writing as early as 1854 and 1855. For example, he printed in the Mansfield *Herald* of October 3, 1855, what was supposedly a letter from J. Augustus Sniggs, which ridiculed the Sag Nichts (Locofocos or Democrats) by pretending to support them, in exactly the same manner that the first signed Nasby letter ridiculed the Democrats (the brackets are Locke's):

NOTE FROM AN UNFLEDGED SAG NICHT

[The following was received too late for insertion, last week. We sympathise with the writer in his mishaps, but assure him that he may if he perseveres, become a bright and shining light in the order.]

Mansfield, Sept. 27, 1855.

EDITORS OF THE HERALD:—I have lived in this dirty world of ours, several years, and supposed that I had seen a little of most everything that was to be seen, considered myself posted in regard to most matters, and have for a long time labored under the hallucination that there were very few men on this mud-ball who could astonish me. Vain man! self-conceited wretch that I am! I find that I'm a baby in pantaloons, a yearling in standing collars, a suckling chewing tobacco, a boy with years on his head. You ask in what particular I have so deceived myself? I answer, in any ideas of politics.

I have been led into this acknowledgment by attending a Sag Nicht meeting—not a regular meeting of the order, but a meeting of their candidates and leaders, for the purpose of devising ways and means, reporting progress, and general consultation. I was introduced by my esteemed friends, Messrs. Brandenoaz and Liteninfas. As we entered the room all business was suspended, I being a stranger to them. My friends assured them it was all right, and to remove all doubts of my devotion to the party pointed at my nose. Each one scrutinized it closely, but seeing that it was of a sufficiently deep red hue, and that the colors were set as fast as logwood brandy could do it, I was welcomed as a brother, at once, and they at once proceeded to business.

First in order came the reports of the candidates, and those who had been out on electioneering tours. The business was conducted in a loose, free and easy manner, each man speaking as the spirit moved. The man in the chair called—but I will mention no names. A little, red-haired, wiry-faced man arose. He had, on an average, three bottles in each pocket, having just returned from the country. Some of them contained Irish

whisky, some schnapps, and the others New England Rum. I
made up my mind that he would be elected. He knew enough
to strike national prejudices in the only vulnerable spot, viz:
in the gullet. "How 'smatters goen?" asked the man in the chair,
in a voice something between a hiccough and a snore. "Well,
good, that is, yes, pretty good," replied the man with the bottles,
"I b'lieve I've got Dutch Dave beat badly." (Just then another
man with bottles in his pocket, cautioned him not to say "Dutch
Dave," or in any way convey the impression that his opponent
was of German descent—it might lose him the foreign vote.
Wiry-face winked acquiescence, and proceeded.) "I've fired,
to-day, my biggest wads at the clean shirted American! [Vocif-
erous cheering.] I told 'em Dutch, 'scuse me, the Deacon lay
drunk all the time, seven days in the week, that all the old
Whigs were going against him, and to clinch the matter I
have promised two deputyships in each township. To make it
perfectly sure, I shall start to-morrow and promise as many
more. I can dodge 'em easy enough, after election." The speaker
took his seat.

The propriety of blackening the characters of the opposing
candidates was then discussed. After some debate, it was finally
decided that course of tactics should be adopted. One remarked
that inasmuch as the election this fall decided their fate for
years, that as not one present—he said it from the most intimate
knowledge of their respective capacities—could make a decent
living out of office, as their very bread and butter depended
upon the coming election, there should be herculean efforts
made to achieve a triumph. Their opponents had all the truth
and all the argument, but gentlemen, (here he warmed up,) I
bullieve we can beattum yet. They havn't got our tactics. Look
at it! They havn't raised a cent to put into the grog holes—they
havn't treated a single sucker in the county. They don't know
how to manage matters. Let us use the same means we have in
years gone by, and the day is ours. My friend last upon the
floor, hit the nail upon the head the first pop. In the bottles
he carries, I see success, in the lies he spreads I see triumph.
I am glad to see him thus vigorously rolling on the Democratic
Ball and lighting up the Democratic fires. [Here the speaker was
interrupted by the chairman, who hinted that inasmuch as the
gentleman wasn't writing an editorial for the Shield and Banner,
and as he was among those with whom clap trap was un-

necessary, he might leave out the Democratic balls and Democratic Fires. It would do well enough among the people, but here—bosh! it made him sick. The speaker proceeded.] I too have been doing my part. I have been telling in two townships that one of the Republican candidates is in the daily practice of whipping his wife. [Applause.] That is the course we must pursue. It's the dodge that tells."

I was then called upon to say something. I commenced by remarking that to me, Democracy was a principle. The candidates all looked at each other and winked—one remarking that it was a devilish good joke. I was indignant at the levity with which they received the word "principle," and I insisted that I meant what I said. The Chairman called me to order, and remarked they had met there for the purpose of transacting business—not to listen to stale jokes. I grew hot, and yelled "Gentlemen I am in earnest—I am struggling for princip"——

I would have went on but just then a square bottle, formerly the local habitation of a familiar spirit called gin, struck me on the left side of the head, and as it came with considerable velocity I fell. Several clutched my collar, others my feet, and amid cries of "Hustle the d---d spy out," "Down stairs with him," "Principles, indeed," I was precipitated into the street. I thought it was hard. I had read the Shield and Banner for a long time, and being naturally credulous, supposed in my innocence that the party to which I belonged really had principles to contend for, and I was not prepared to be fully undeceived. It was wrong in Brandenoaz and Liteninfas to let me into the whole secret at once. They should have broken it to me by degrees.

I am still a Democrat, and shall so continue. The flight down those stairs, sudden and unexpected as it was, hasn't shook my attachment to the party. It was done hastily, and was disagreeable to me, but I can make allowances. They were undoubtedly excited at the sound of the obnoxious word I made use of.

Having discovered my error, I think I can now hold my own among the Sag Nichts. To prove to them my sincerity and earnestness I shall start to-morrow electioneering, and have accordingly provided myself with a five gallon keg of liquor and a copy of Munchausen. The first I shall dispense freely, and the second I shall humbly endeavor to imitate. Whether it will make votes or lose them I know not, but these are the tools they are using, and they cannot blame me for following their example. My father was a Democrat, and if he was alive now, would be a Sag Nicht, and my being kicked down stairs on suspicion shall not eradicate his teachings.

Respectfully,

J. AUGUSTUS SNIGGS.

In 1858 and 1859 Locke interested himself in the literary burlesque, producing "The Bow-Legged Knight," a burlesque romance in the Bucyrus *Journal* for October 29, 1858; and several "sonnits," for example, "2 a Skeeter" by P. Nutts, in the *Journal* for July 9, 1859; and "Tu Whiski," reprinted in the Cleveland *Plain Dealer* for August 11, 1859. These were later published in *Divers Views, Opinions, and Prophecies of Petroleum V. Nasby*. The romance was originally in normal spelling and had passable grammar, with the single exception of the line "Marguerite was kum 2." But the sonnets were early experiments with comic misspelling and other ludicrous illiteracies. The *Plain Dealer* sonnet, as it originally appeared, will illustrate:

Sonnit—Tu Whiski
By a Admirer uv the Beveridge—Ritten imejitly After takin a nip, the labor interspersed with Ockashunil Wettin my lips with the same.

Whiski! all hale! from erlyist boyhood, I
Heve ardently admyred this qwalities.
Thowst clothed mi mind with strength—mi nos in richest dyer.
Hale! whiski, hale! potent son of Ry!*
When wus grows wus, the bad grows badder,
When trubbul's wave across my bussum roll,
A nip of the expands mi shrunken sole,
As wind from boys mouth expands a bladder.†
Water is good—no man of sens denies it
Serch thru old Nacher, and you will not meet
An artikle so fit for washing feet. ††
But as a Beveridge, faw, their i dispised it;
Mi stummic turns, and for relief i fli
To the eckstract uv corn—to the Red Eye.

*Aluding to the plesent fikshun that whiski is maid uv ry which is not by no menes; on the contrary ub korn.

† A butiful similie, appropritly chosen to show the elickser uv life will cos a man to spread hisself.

†† The liberality uv this centiment is noble, it is grand.— While assertin the superioriti uv his favorite beveridge, he is willin to allow that sum us kin be maid uv uther likwids. Such noble mindedness is refreshin.

Another item in the Bucyrus *Journal* antedated the first letter over the signature of Petroleum V. Nasby, and that was "Secession in a New Spot," the mock editorial of December 13, 1860, that ridiculed Southern sympathizers of Crawford County. In it Locke's sarcasm was at its best; the arguments for secession were reduced to absurdity in the supposed attempt to acclaim them. The true Nasbyan pose was here. It required only the addition of Nasby's language and spelling and the changing of the name of Bucyrus to transform the list of grievances into the opening Nasby letter in *Divers Views* in 1865. According to the editorial, Crawford County proclaimed to the world its independence from Ohio and the United States, following the lead of South Carolina, and the words echoed the pattern of the Declaration of Independence:

... Our whole history has been one of aggression on the part of the State.

It refused to locate the Capitol at Bucyrus, to the great detriment of our real estate owners.

It refused to gravel the streets of Bucyrus, or even re-lay the plank road.

It refused to locate the Penitentiary at Bucyrus, notwithstanding we do as much towards filling it as any other county.

It refused to locate the State Fair at Bucyrus, thus blighting the hopes of our free, independent and patriotic pea-nut venders.

It located the Ohio Canal one hundred miles east of Bucyrus. . . .

The Sniggs letters, the burlesques, and the mock editorial were but previews of the real Nasby letters, which burst full blown upon the public in 1862, not long after Locke's removal to Findlay, Ohio. The first appearance of the name of Nasby was in the "Letter from a Straight Democrat" in the Findlay *Hancock Jeffersonian* for April 25, 1862. Many years later, Locke explained the immediate circumstances of its origin:

About the time the war broke out, I heard of a paper being circulated for signatures, petitioning the Legislature to prohibit negroes from coming into the state, and asking for legislation to remove all the colored population the state then contained. What was known as Copperheadism was an important element in the state political history of the time.

I was then, as now, a Republican, and the petition was not brought to me. I heard of it, and hearing also that it was being circulated by a shiftless, worthless fellow, named Levi Flenner,—whose parents, by the way, were both in the almshouse as county charges,—I made up my mind to see that paper. The satire of the situation struck me at once. The few negroes we had in Findlay were hard-working, law-abiding men, and to remove them and leave Levi was a preposterous outrage upon the fitness of things.

One night, in a drug store, where people gather in country towns, I met Levi. I saw a paper in his pocket, and, as I knew the fellow never read a newspaper at all, I seized it as the petition. And so it was. I read it aloud with comments, and as I read, interpolating my own remarks, I felt the afflatus of the situation and made up my mind to write the Nasby letters. That week I published the first one.[5]

The original characters, situations, and places in the Nasby letters were real people, incidents, and localities in the vicinity of Findlay. Their significance was local and timely. In the later collected editions, Findlay was changed to Wingert's Corners, and the names of the characters were changed or omitted. The first use of the name Wingert's Corners in the original newspaper letters was in the June 12, 1863, issue of the *Jeffersonian;* and by that time Locke probably realized that he had something of national significance in Nasby. The first Nasby letter, however, was supposedly a letter to the editor of the *Jeffersonian,* and was designed to demolish Levi Flenner and the signers of his petition:

[74]

The Reverse Logic of Petroleum V. Nasby

LETTER FROM A STRAIGHT DEMOCRAT.

ED JEFF.—the follerin petishun, the ijee uv wich wuz sejested bi me hez bin cirkelated in Finlay, durin the past week:

"We, the undersigned, voters of Hancock county, Ohio, in view of the intimation made by the President of the United States, in his message, that by an act of Congress, and by the laws of the States, to be hereafter enacted, many of the negroes, held as slaves, may be set at liberty, and fearing that they may wander into Ohio, much to the detriment of the white inhabitants of our State, and especially to those who have to depend upon their labor to support themselves and families:

We, therefore, respectfully ask your honorable body to pass a law as stringent in its provisions as totally to prohibit any negroes from immigrating into, settling, or holding property in Ohio."

I adress you on the subgik becoz I want to reech Republikins. Democrasy is all rite on this question. Republikins is not, therfour thems the 1s ime after. I kum 2 bring sinners not rightchus men to repentans.

There is now fifteen niggers, men, wimen and children, or ruther, mail, femail and yung, in Finlay, and yisterday, another arove. I am bekoming alarmed, fur ef thay increse at this rate, in suthin over sixty yeres they'll hev a majority in the town, and may, ef thay git mene enuff, tirranize over us, even ez we air tirranizin over them. The danger is imminent! Alreddy our poor white inhabitans is out of employment to maik room for that nigger—even now our shops and factories is full uv that nigger, to the great detriment uv a white inhabitant who hez a family to support, and our county Infirmry is full uv him.

I imploar the peepul to wake up. Let us hold a mass meetin to taik this subgik into considerashun, and thet bisness may be expedited, I perpose the passig uv a series uv preamble and resolushens suthin like the follerin, to-wit, viz:

Wareas, we vew with alarm the ackshun uv the Presydent uv the U. S., in recommendin the imejit emansipashun uv the slaves uv owr misgided suthrin breethren, and his evident intenshun uv kolonising on em in Ohio, and the heft on em in Hankok county, and

Wareas, in the event uv this imigrashun owr fello townman Levi g. Flenner and uthers hooz families depend upon thare labor fur support wood be throde owt uv employment and

Wareas, wen you giv a man a hoss you air obleeged to also make him a present uv a silver plated harness and a $200 buggy, so ef we let the nigger live here we air in duty bound to let him vote, and to marry him off hand, and

Wareas, wen this stait uv affares ariv our pore stait will be no fit plais for men uv edjucashun and refinement, and

Wareas, any man hevin the intellek uv a brass mounted jackass kin esily see that the 2 raisis want never intended to live together, and

Wareas, we see in the futur much trubble arisin out uv this complikasion, and

Wareas, bein in the majority we kin do ez we plese, and ez the nigger aint no vote he cant help hisself therefore be it

Resolved, that the crude, un deodorized afrikan, is a disgustin objik

Resolved, that this convenshun, wen it hez its feet washed, smells sweeter nor the afrikan in his normal* condishun, and is thair4 his superior.

Resolved, the niggers be druv out uv Finley.

Resolved, that sech property ez tha may hev akkumulated be confistikated and the proseeds applide to the follerin purposes, to wit viz namely:

1 Pament uv the bils uv the last Dimekratik central komitte.

2 Pament of the disenterested patriots ez cirkelated the abuv petishun.

3 The balenz to remane in mi hanz to be used next ortum fer perlitikel perpusses.

Resolved, that the Republicans who oppose these resorlutions all wanter marry a nigger.

Resolved, that Dr. Carlin in rentin a part uv his bildin to 2 afrikens hez struck a blo at the very foundashuns uv sosiety.

Resolved, that in that artikle uv the constitooshun that reeds "all men air created free an equil," the wurds "ceptin niggers," shood be addid too wunst.

Fello whites, arous! The inemy is onto us! Our harths is in danger! Wen we hev a nigger fer judg—niggers fur teechers—niggers in pulpits—wen niggers rule and controle sosiety, then will you remember this warnin! Arowse to wunst!

Rally aginst Conway!

Rally aginst Hegler!

Rally aginst Hegler's family!

Rally aginst the porter at the Reed House!
Rally aginst the cook at the Crook House!
Rally aginst the nigger widder in Vance's addishun!
Rally aginst the nigger that cum yisterday!
Rally aginst the saddle-culord girl that used to be hear!
Amerika fur wite men!

PETROLEUM V. NASBY.

Jest west uv Finley, Aprile the 20, 18sixty too.

*I don't jest no wat "Normal" menes, but I seen it in the Nu York Da Buk [the *Day Book,* a Democratic newspaper], so it must be a sound dimecratic word.

II *Theme*

Of course, Petroleum V. Nasby was more than a caricature of an individual. He represented a type familiar in the Midwest and especially in Ohio during the Civil War years, and he came to represent for Locke and many of his readers the typical Democrat. He was obviously an exaggeration, with no redeeming features. His "logic" was always absurd, his statements of "fact" were gross lies, his opinions were motivated solely by self-interest. Like Sut Lovingood, he was a rascal; but he was a thorough rascal—one with whom we could never be in sympathy. Indeed, Locke's basic method of satire was the utter blackening of the opposition.

Except in the earliest Nasby letters which were later revised, Nasby's places of residence were likewise symbolic. The change from Findlay to "Wingert's Corners" was Locke's acknowledgment of the greater significance of the place. Wingert's Corners represented the hopelessly provincial crossroads where the illiterate peasantry indulged in misbegotten dreams of grandeur. After the Civil War, Nasby moved from Ohio to the more hospitable border state of Kentucky, where he settled in Confedrit X Roads. The new locale represented, for Locke, the typical village in the unreconstructed South. Here Nasby remained for the rest of his days, except for occasional periods of travel and his brief residence in New York.

The friends and neighbors of Nasby at Confedrit X Roads were also types, who appeared regularly in the letters from

1865 to the end, in 1887. The dominating figure was George Washington Bascom, the saloonkeeper, who owned mortgages on all the surrounding land because of the residents' unquenchable thirst for liquor and unchangeable aversion to working for a living. The "elite uv the Corners" were Elkanah Pogram, Kernel Hugh McPelter, and Squire Gavitt and their families, former landowners and slave owners. They had the vices of Nasby without the sharpness; and, since they could neither read nor write, they were ready to believe anything Nasby told them to the detriment of the "ablishnists" of the North. The real heroes of the letters were Pollock, the storekeeper from Illinois, and Joseph Bigler, a Confederate veteran who had learned his lesson and wanted to improve the conditions of the South. But Pollock and Bigler were able to do little more than harass the oldtimers. There was never much improvement in the Crossroads, and pre-war attitudes remained adamant.

Locke's method of characterization was broad and simple, and consisted almost entirely of letting the characters speak for themselves, while an occasional line of narrative pointed out the discrepancies between their words and their actions. The following lines, for example, characterized both Pollock and Mrs. Pogram:

"Mrs. P.," sed this Illinoy store-keeper, wich his name it wuz Pollock, "do yoo object to miscegenation?"

"Missee—what?" replied she, struck all uv a heap at the word.

"Miscegenation—amalgamation—marryin whites with niggers."

"Do I?" retorted she; "ketch a son uv mine marryin a nigger! They are another race; they'r beasts; and who'd marry em but jist sich men ez Sumner and them other Ablishnists?"

"Then permit me to ask," sed this Pollock, wich wuz bound to kick up a muss, "ef ther's any race uv pure blood in this section uv Kentucky wich is yaller?"

"No! uv course not," sed Mrs. P.; "them yaller people is mulatters—half nigger, half white. . . ."

"And no Kentuckian ever marries a nigger?" inquired the store-keeper, who I saw wuz pursooin his investigations altogether too far.

"Never!" sed Mrs. Pogram; "we leave that to Ablishnists."

"Well, then," sed this Pollock, who, I spect, wuzn't half so innsent ez he let on, "I see that yoo hev no objection to mixin with the nigger, providin yoo don't do it legally; that amalgama- shen don't hurt nothin, pervidin yoo temper it with adultery. Is that the idee, Mrs. Pogram?"[6]

None of the characters was realistic or well rounded. Each existed for a single purpose and to illustrate a type. Nasby himself had but two dimensions; any further development would be likely to make us sympathetic and thus destroy the propaganda effect. There were no in-betweens; a character was either all good or all bad.

The theme of the letters was always political and always Republican. Whether Nasby was talking about abolition, re- construction, prohibition, women's rights, free trade, or the merits of particular public figures, Locke's ulterior aim was to stigmatize the Democratic Party and, by implication, to move the reader to the Republican point of view: "Humanity in the United States is divided into two classes—them ez wear clean shirts and sox, and—Dimocrats."[7] Defectors from Republicanism were treated with little more respect than were Democrats. In the elections of 1872 and 1884, when many erstwhile Republicans deserted the party because of the corruptions discovered within it, Locke ridiculed the deserters by making Nasby welcome them. In his letter of November 24, 1871, Nasby said: "I . . . accept the passive policy, and am convinst that the Dimocrisy shood not, as a party, nominate a candidate for the Presidency, but shel, to save the country from impendin rooin, relinquish their party organizashen, and co-operate with sich uv the Republikins ez are dissatisfied with the [Grant] Administrashen and innoggerate a reign uv purity."[8] And the letter ended with the citizens of Confedrit X Roads unanimously recommending Jefferson Davis as the coalition candidate for president.

III *Form*

With few exceptions, the Nasby letters fell into six patterns: the narrative of Nasby's escapades, the interview, the dream, the proceedings of a meeting, the "wail," and the editorial monologue. The narrative pattern permitted the widest variety and provided a framework of continuity, such as it was, for the whole series of letters. In the narrative letters, we learn of Nasby's desertion to the Confederacy and his escape to Canada during the Civil War, of his flight to New Jersey before settling in Kentucky, of his tour as chaplain with Andrew Johnson, of his adventures as a wildcat banker, and of his electioneering in Ohio and Indiana. In the letter of November 1, 1862, for example, Nasby told of his arrival at the camp of the "Loosiana Pelicans," where he was confronted by the colonel:

"Mr. Nasby, I reseeve you gladly ez a recroot in the Grand Army uv Freedom. Ez yoo divest yoorself uv the clothes uv the tyrant, divest yerself uv whatever lingrin affecshuns yoo may hev fer the land uv yer nativity, and ez yoo array yorself in the garb uv a Suthrin soljer, try to fill yer sole with that Suthrin feelin that animates us all. Jones," sed he, addressin his orderly, "is Thompson dead yit?"

"Not quite," sez the orderly.

"Never mind," sez the kernel, "he cant git well uv that fever; strip off his uniform and give it to Nasby, and berry him."

I judgd, from the style uv uniforms I saw on the men around me, that I wood rather keep my own, but I sed nothin. When the orderly returned with the deceest Thompson's uniform, I groaned innardly. There wuz a pair uv pants with the seat entirely torn away, and wun leg gone below the knee, a shoe with the sole off, and the straw he had wrapped around the other foot, and a gray woolen shirt. Sez the kernel:

Don't be afeered uv me, Nasby. Put on yer uniform rite here."

Reluctantly, I pulled off my new dubble-soled boots, and I wuz petrified to see the kernel kick off the slippers he wore, and pull em on. I pulled off my pants—he put em on, and so on with every article uv dress I possest, even to my warm overcoat and blankit. Sez the kernel:

"These articles, Nasby, belongs to the Guvment, to which I shel akount for them. Report yoorself to-wunst to Captin Smith."

Ez I passed out, the lootenant-kernel, majer, and adjutent pulled me to wun side, and askt me "ef I coodent git three more to desert." Wun glance at their habillyments showd why they wuz so anxious fer deserters.[9]

Each narrative letter was a story in itself with its own satirical thrust, and in addition it often forwarded the plot of the Nasby letters as a whole. On the other hand, the incidents were often repetitious and sometimes contradictory. Accounts of Nasby's marriage occurred four times in the course of the letters[10]—as early as the letter of November 11, 1862, and as late as that of February 5, 1881—and, while some of the details were redundant, others were inconsistent. But Nasby never remained in the married state for long, and the inconsistencies were not important to the overall effect. As a matter of fact, plot in the Nasby letters was merely a device to add interest to the individual pieces and to string together the series. There was no development of character and no progress toward a grand climax. Things were about the same at the conclusion of the series as at the beginning. Nasby had learned nothing; indeed, he had not even aged over the twenty-six years of his newspaper correspondence.

Locke made frequent use of the pattern of the interview to ridicule his political enemies. In July of 1863, he had Nasby interview Clement L. Vallandigham, the Ohio Copperhead who had been banished for sedition by the Lincoln administration two months earlier:

"Marterd saint!" sez I, with a voice tremulous with emoshen.

"Sufferer fer truth!" sez he; and then this trooly grate man whispered, "Jest keep in this posishn a minnit—the artist uv the Noo York Illustratid Flapdoodle is makin a sketch uv us;" wich we did, standin locked into each other's arms, and weepin profoosely fer 15 minits. It wuz exhaustin and tiresome, but for the cause I endoored it. The picter will appear in next week's Flapdoodle, headed "The Two Grate Minds uv the Age! Affectin meeting uv Vallandigum and Nasby!" The matter akompanying the picter will be written by Vallandigum and myself—he writin wat relates to hisself, and I wat relates to myself. We kin do ourselves justis.

"Nasby," says the great C. L., "how is things in my native state?"

"Squally," sez I.

"Wat was the pervalin sentiment uv the people as to my eggsile?"

"They wuz extremely glad uv it."

"The akount uv my prostrashen—my untold suffrins, et settry, wich I hed publisht in the papers; did that not affect them?"

"Yes; they laft."

"Did not the affectin akount uv the wife uv my buzm and my cherub babes a jinin me here, to share my lonely eggsile, move em?"

"Nary move."

"Nasby, the peeple is stun. But I'll fetch em. 'Nil despritrando' is my motto. I must be guvner, fer how else kin we prevent the subjugashen uv the Dimekratik staits? Elect me, and ther'll be no trouble about drafts, onless we shood git involved in a war with the United States. The Confederacy wood be recognized, Ohio wood go with the South, and slavery wood be interdoost, and ez we woodent hev any further use fer em, poor men woodent be allowed to vote, making me perpetooal guvner. Nasby, we must succeed."[11]

In his time, Nasby interviewed Andrew Johnson, Jefferson Davis, Winfield S. Hancock, Samuel J. Tilden, as well as several fictitious personages and even the devil himself, who "threw his left arm about my neck in a extasy uv irrepressible love." He visited President Abraham Lincoln, too, who patiently allowed Nasby to exude his advice and wryly told him he would "give the matter serious considerashen."

Mr. Nasby's dreams were always allegorical, prophetic, or admonitory. He dreamed of the spirit of Andrew Jackson returning to haunt those who had vitiated the Democratic Party. He had a vision of the next world, where the leaders of the Democrats tried to cross the Jordan to Heaven but were weighted down by their sins. He imagined the corpse of the giant Republicanism, killed by the Johnson administration, coming back to life upon getting a breath of fresh air from the North. He envisioned a horse race, in which the Democratic entry showed great promise until it was overburdened with the planks of the party platform. During the presidential campaign of 1864, which put Lincoln in office for a second term, he imagined himself visiting an American schoolroom two hundred years hence:

The school-marm wuz eggsaminin a class uv youngsters in history.

"Who wuz the greatest and goodest men the Yoonitid Staits ever prodoost?"

"George Washington and Aberham Linkin."

"What did they do?"

"Washington founded the goverment, and Linkin preserved it."

"Who wuz the wust men the country prodoost?"

A little girl ansed:

"Joodath Ithcariot, Benedict Arnold, Jeff Davith, and Vallandigum."

"Yoo are wrong, my child," retorted the school-marm. "Judas lived in another country, and before the others. They were so simler, however, that the error is excoosible. What did Arnold, and Davis, and Vallandigum do?"

"Arnold betrayed his country, and took up arms agin it; Davis rebelled agin his goverment, and Vallandigum helped him all he cood without gettin hisself into danger."

"What names were given them ez opposed the goverment in '76 and '61?"

"Tories and Copperheads."

"Which wuz the wust, the Tories or Copperheads?"

"That pint hez bin much discussed, but no concloosion hez ever bin arriv at."

"How many times wuz Linkin elected President?"

"Two."

"Had he any opposition for the second term?"

"None to speak uv. The rebels and Copperheads run a disgraced soljer, whose name sum historians giv ez Mickfadden, uthers ez Micknellan, and uthers ez Micklellan; but ez he receeved no votes in the electoral colledge, the eleckshun wuz considered unanimus. The Copperhead candidate sunk into obskoority after the war, and he wuz forgotten, wich wuz lucky for his children. . . ."

I awoke from this dream in a cold sweat. "Is it possible," thot I, "that posterity will so regard us?" and for a minnit I wuz almost persuadid to be a Christian. But I thot uv the post-offisis, and sed to myself, "What is posterity to a ded man? Let me hev offis, and the means uv keepin my skin full uv whisky, without work, and posterity may think wot it pleases."[12]

The most common means of public entertainment in the small communities of the Midwest was the political and religious meetings. Nasby exploited both for his ignominious ends on every possible occasion. As self-appointed pastor of the Church of St. Vallandigham, later the Church uv the Noo Dispensashun, he maintained spiritual control of his flock; and, as the only person in the community who could read and write, he called and presided at most of the political rallies. The reports of the meetings consisted of either Reverend Nasby's sermons—which were always of political import—or of the resolutions that he persuaded his followers to pass. A frequent diversion resulted from the breaking up of the meeting by some unforeseen incident which disrupted Nasby's plans; and the incident was most often brought on by the gadflies Bigler and Pollock. In July, 1866, the trouble-maker was a sergeant connected with the Freedman's Bureau, who interrupted Nasby's sermon on the prodigal son:

"My brethren," sed I, "sich uv yoo ez hev Bibles in yoor houses, kin get somebody to read yoo the parable to wich I shel call yoor attention. A man, wunst upon a time, hed sons, ez many men hev since, and wun uv em wuz a tough one, who hed a taste for that pertikeler branch uv agriculture known ez sowin wild oats. He left his home and went into far countries, makin the old man shel out his share uv the estate, and he lived high, jist, my brethren, ez yoor boys do, or rather, did, when they went to Noo Orleans, in the days when yoo hed a nigger or two wich yoo cood sell to supply em with money. He played draw poker and faro; he drank fancy drinks, and boarded at big hotels; and he follered after strange women, which'll bust a man quicker nor any one small sin the devil hez yet invented, ez yoor pastor kin testify. Uv course, his pile give out, and he got down, my friends, did this ingenuous yooth, to rags and wretchedness, and ended in being an overseer uv swine. What did he do? He ariz and went to his father, and the old man saw him afar off, and went out to meet him, and fell onto his neck, and give him a order for a suit of clothes and a pair uv boots, and put a ring onto his finger, and made a feast, killin for the purpose the fatted calf wich he hed saved for another occasion.

"My friends, you kin find in the Skripter suthin applicable to every occasion, and this parable fits the present time like a ready-made coat. The South is the Prodigal Son. We went out from our father's house on a expedition wich hezn't proved altogether a success. We spent our share uv the estate, and a little more. We run through our means, and hev cum down to rags, and dirt, and filth, and hunger. We are, and hev bin some time, a chawin husks. We run out after them twin harlots, Slavery and State Rights, and they've cleaned us out. Our pockets are empty. No more doth the pleasant half-dollar jingle in sweet unison agin its fellows. Our wallets is barren uv postal currency, and the grocery-keepers mourn, and refuse to be comforted, becoz we are not. We hev got to the husk stage uv our woe, and wood be tendin hogs, ef the armies, wich past through these countries, hed left us any. We hev come back. In rags and dirt we hev wended our way to Washington, and ask to be taken back. Now, why don't our father, the Government, fulfil the Skripter: Why don't it see us afar off, and run out to meet us? Why don't it put onto us a purple robe? Where's the ring for our finger, and the shoes for our feet? and where's the fatted calf he ought to kill? My brethren, them Ablishnists is worse than infiddles—while they preach the gospel they won't practise it. For my part, I——"

At this point a sargent, belongin to that infernal Burow, who wuz in the audience, with enough uv soldiers to make opposin uv him unpleasant, sed he hed bin a sort uv an exhorter in his day, and desired to say a word in explanation uv that parable, ez applicable to the present time; and, sez he, "ef I am interrupted, remember I b'long to the church military, wich is, just now, the church triumphant." And cockin his musket he proceeded, very much uninterrupted. . . .

"The Prodigal Son went out,—so did the South,—thus farly the cases is alike.

"The Prodigal didn't steal nothin. The Confederacy took everything it cood lay its hands on.

"The Prodigal spent only what wuz his to spend. The Confederacy spent not only all it stole, but all it cood borrer, when it knowed its promises to pay wuzent worth the mizable paper they wuz printed onto.

"The Prodigal, when he did come, come ez penitent ez the consciousness that he hed made a fool uv hisself cood make him. The Confederacy wuz whipped back, but it still swears hefty oaths that it wuz right all the time.

"The Prodigal didn't *demand* veal pot-pies, and purple robes, and sich, but begged to be a servant unto the more sensible brethren wich stayed. The South comes back *demandin* office, uv wich the fatted calf, and rings, and purple robes is typical, and considerably more share in the government than it had before it kicked over the traces, and went out. . . .

"I am anxious to kill that fatted calf, and am also anxious to put on yoo robes and shoes. But, alas! the calf suffered from want uv attention so long doorin the late misunderstandins that he's too poor—the robes wuz all cut up into bloo kotes for the soljers we sent out to fetch yoo in—the shoes they wore out, and the rings—Jeff'son Davis wears the only style we hev. When you come back in good shape, yool find us ready to meet yoo; but till then, chaw husks?"[13]

In the dark days of the Democratic Party, between the elections of Lincoln in 1860 and Grover Cleveland in 1884, there were many occasions for Petroleum V. Nasby to despair. And, being a minister, he frequently expressed his despair in a "wail" or lamentation, based upon the style of the Book of Job, the Psalms, or the Lamentations. At rare intervals his Biblical parodies took the form of a psalm of rejoicing, chiefly during the administration of Johnson. But much more often he was "a kittle full of cusses." His letter of May 16, 1864, expressed his despondency at Northern military victories and at the hopeless situation of the Democratic leaders: Vallandigham; Fernando Wood, the mayor of New York; and George B. McClellan, the Democratic candidate for president in the forthcoming election.

Lift up yer voices mournfly, O my people!

Howl, O ye saints! howl like unto the hungry wolf and the disapinted jackal.

Cry out like wun who hath a great pain—like him who suffreth with belly-ake.

Cast ashes upon yer head, O Fernandywood, and clothe yerself in sack-cloth.

Hev another colleckshun taken up, O Vallandigum, and pay yer board a year or two in advance, for yer exel is lengthened.

Weep and wale, and gnash yer teeth, O Dimokrasy, for yoo hev bin measured, and yer coffin ordered, and the day uv yer funeral apinted; and lo! the corpse will be ready.

For the biter hez bin bit; yea, the strong man hez bin overcome.

Grant, who wuz to hev bin whipt, wuz not whipt; on the contrary, quite the reverse.

And Lee, him we sot our harts upon, hez bin beaten, and grate hez bin the slawter uv his host.

And Beast Butler will take Richmond, and will not be hangd, ez we prayd.

And the Confedracy will be strangled, and Linkin will be President, and the offisis will be lost to us forever and forever.

Uv wat avale to us wuz Fort Piller, or Plymouth, or Red River? Lo! they were but flea-bites on the back uv a giant.

For in Virginny hev we bin chawed up egrejis.

And our week-kneed wuns, them ez wantid peace last month, hev become blud-thirsty, and hooror for Linkin.

Wale, ye saints!

For we hev chained ourselves to a corpse, and the corpse stinketh.

Die, O Micklellan, for yoo woodent sell at the rate uv a dollar a dozen, ef playd-out genrals wuz in demand.

Thou, too, O Vallandigum, for yer marterdum woodent win.

Steel viggerusly, O Fernandywood, for it's yer last chance.

For wen the grate South fiddled did we not alluz dance? and now that she dieth, shall we not go and do likewise?[14]

Finally, many of the Nasby letters were apparently straightforward expressions of Nasby's opinions—editorials. Actually, of course, these "editorials" were burlesques of Democratic opinion. Sometimes Nasby exhorted the people to action, as in "Appeal to the Democracy" (October 4, 1865); sometimes he analyzed the political situation, as in "Fremont's Nomination" (June 2, 1864); and sometimes he proposed a political stratagem. An illustration of such a proposal was the letter of January 20, 1877, in which he suggested a means of settling the disputed election of the previous November so that his candidate, Samuel J. Tilden, would win over Hayes:

I most hartily endorse the plan for leavin out the Presidenshel question to a jint commishn to be made up from the Senit and the House, and the Supreme court, the members uv the latter to be determined by lot. This thing uv injectin the element uv chance into a game wher yoor opponent hez ded-wood on yoo, is pleasant and very kind. By doin this we are playin on even terms, the Republikins furnishin all the stakes. A gambler wich woodn't take such chances is not worthy uv the name.

By this plan the Presidency is made a matter uv chance. All I ask now is a slite change in the method. Under the jint committee's plan, ef we are lucky enuff to git the odd member uv the Soopreme court, Tilden and reform goes in, and I git my postoffis. I am trustin my fortunes to the blind goddiss. Ef it is to be made a matter uv chance wat is the yoose of worryin so many men? Two kin decide it ez well ez a dozen, and instid uv hevin so many I beg to make the follerin sejestions:

1. That the Dimocrisy elect a strictly representative Dimocrat, and the Republikins a strikly representative Republikin, with two umpires and the bottle holder, wich shel be me.

2. That them two set down, and play seven-up, yooker, or the more muskeler game uv freeze out, to determine whether Tilden and reform or Hayes and oppression, shel be President for the next four yeers.

3. The two representative men may determine for theirselves the game and its condishens. Ef freeze-out, they may make the amount ez large or ez small as they choose; ef eny other game, they may make it the best two in three, the best three in five, or the best four in seven, or the first fifty-one in a hundred, or any way they may choose, so that they get thro by the 4th uv March. I shoodn't want the struggle to run longer than that, for the biznis interests uv the Corners is sufferin. My bill at Bascom's is runnin up enormously, and ez I owe all the citizens, trade is blocked till I git the postoffis, so ez to pay suthin, and put money into cirkelashen. I must hev that postoffis soon or perish, or else bankrupt Bascom.

4. The winner to name the President, and the people to acquiesce without a murmur.[15]

These six forms were the patterns for nearly all of the Nasby letters as published in *The Struggles of Petroleum V. Nasby* and *The Nasby Letters*. Occasionally the forms were mixed, as when an editorial concluded with a narrative of happenings or when a sermon merged with a wail. In the earlier letters, Nasby now and then broke out in verse—the "sonnit" was his favorite form, though there were also "oads" and "laments." The "Sonnit—2 a Litter uv Little Pigs" was among the best of these effusions. Printed in *Divers Views, Opinions, and Prophecies,* it was omitted from the *Struggles.*

> Root on! root on! ye sportiv little pigs!
>   Ah! cood ye uv the fucher hev a site,
>   Yoor little tails wood not kurl up so tite,
> But droop despondin down yoor hinder legs.
> Yoo live o'erwell—uv food yoo hev no lack;
>   But 'tis not luv that gives yoo daily swill—
>   'Tis not the promptins uv a gen'rus will—
> Yoor karkasis must pay the trubble back;
> Yoo'll all kum 2 it when yoor sumwhat fatter,
> Stuck, dressed, and served up, roasted on a platter.
> As shoor ez fate the unfeelin butcher's steel
> Will cut yoor windpipe, spite uv kick or squeal.
> [Here cums in the moral, wich wuz segested by my borrerin
> munny wunst at ten per cent., givin a mortgage on a farm, and
> renooin till the farm wuz eaten up.]
>   Yoo'll tred the path so old and so well beaten,
>   Fed first by man, and then by mankind eaten!

There were also in the earlier works, but not reproduced in the *Struggles* or the *Letters,* a few tales, such as "The Wise Old Rat," in *Divers Views,* that was later revised and published in *The Morals of Abou Ben Adhem.* And "The Bow-Legged Knite," in *Divers Views,* could rank with the burlesque novels of Artemus Ward and Bret Harte in mocking the incredible plots and the irresponsible morals of popular fiction. Nasby added the following to the end of his story: "Singler ez it may appear to the reader, the above beautiful tale wuz rejected by the conseetid editors of the *Atlantic Monthly!* I wuz not born in Boston."

But the verse and tales were not properly a part of the Nasby saga. The unity and consistency of the letters as a whole depended on the restriction of form and the unvarying political motive. Unfortunately, these restrictions also make for monotony;

even the fertility of Locke's imagination could hardly keep up the interest of a reader who would insist on reading the Nasby letters from beginning to end. This monotony would not be noticed, however, if the letters were read as they were intended to be read: as separate though related pieces of entertaining timely propaganda.

IV *Technique*

A study of Locke's techniques in the Nasby letters must begin with the obvious question of his use of comic misspelling. That device has called down on him the scorn of many a modern critic who lacks the patience to see what is beneath it. It was primarily an attention-getting device, and was just as popular in the middle-nineteenth century as it is now unpopular among scholarly commentators. Josh Billings began his rise to fame by rewriting his "Essay on the Mule" in bad spelling. In the case of the Nasby letters, of course, the device emphasized Nasby's ignorance and gave the reader a strong sense of superiority, no matter how unlearned the reader was himself. Nasby's spelling was not consistent. He would spell the same word both correctly and incorrectly in the same sentence. It has been pointed out that he spelled "Democracy" fifteen different ways in a hundred pages.[16] Furthermore, he was often able to spell perfectly such difficult words as "perquisites," "thermometer," and "ejaculated," but he could not master "have," "been," and "of." There may be some truth in the contention that the misspellings were a convenience arising from Locke's habit of writing the letters directly from the type cases without proofreading. But at least one longhand manuscript exists that shows evidence that Locke did some revising before he published.[17] It is worth noting that Nasby spelled better in the late 1860's and thereafter than he did in the earliest letters, written at the peak of the misspelling fad. Moreover the early letters themselves were partially "corrected" for later book publication.

Of course, the unorthodox spellings often indicated dialect pronunciation. What dialect Locke was imitating has never been investigated, but there is no reason to believe that he took any pains toward accurate recording. It is fair to suppose, both from Nasby's fictitious residence and from Locke's actual residence at the time the Nasby letters were begun, that the dialect was the Northern Midland of central Ohio. But there seems to be no clear-cut difference between the language of Nasby and that of the Kentuckians at Confedrit X Roads. Locke probably aimed at a dialect that would represent uneducated American English generally, and in this he succeeded. We do not think of Nasby as representing a specific region but as representing the semi-literate American.

The Nasby letters rely for their effect on a single overriding technique: sarcasm. Irony is not a strong enough word. Locke's method was blunt and simple, and any other technique that he might use was subsidiary to this. Though Petroleum V. Nasby surely grew out of the tradition of American humor, both he and his letters were virtually humorless. If humor depends on a sympathy with human nature and a recognition of one's own ridiculousness, the reader will look for it in vain in the Nasby letters. Nasby expressed Locke's view of human nature when he said "that seven-tenths uv mankind is bad in a greater or less degree; that the devil hez a warranty deed on four-tenths, a quit-claim to two-tenths, and a mortgage on another tenth. Them in which he hez a present or prospective interest are very largely in the majority."[18] Nor is "wit" the precise word to characterize the Nasby letters. Although Locke's twisting of logic and his manipulation of fact showed undoubted intellectual skill, he wholly lacked the subtlety and spriteliness usually associated with the witty. His aim was entirely destructive; his weapon, a bludgeon.

He never desisted in pounding away at the Democratic Party whether in victory or defeat. If he could have succeeded in annihilating it, then the Nasby papers would have had no reason to continue; but, fortunately for their continuance, the cause did not die. "I remember," said Nasby, "a anti-slavery speaker wich wuz perfoundly greeved when Linkin abolished slavery. 'Great Hevins!' he exclaimed, 'what did he ever do that fur? Wat shel I do now for a coz?'"[19] In the politics of the 1860's and 1870's, Locke never really lacked a cause, yet the effectiveness of the letters depended on the intensity of the political issues involved. The letters were most interesting when the cause they were dealing with was clearest; they were least interesting when the issues were muddled or unimportant. This partly explains their rapid decline in popularity after their author's death: the appeal was no longer timely. It also helps explain why the early letters, dealing with the Civil War and Reconstruction, are still the most readable. The issues involved in those letters are still significant.

But let it be said, Locke was not concerned with immortality in the Nasby papers: "Posterity may assign me a niche in the temple uv massive intellex, or may not; it's all one to the subscriber. I woodn't give a ten-cent postal currency for wat the next generashen will do for me. It's this generashen I'm goin for."[20] The Nasby letters were but a sideline in the busy life of David Ross Locke. He recognized their publicity value and continued to write them for that reason, but he would have preferred to be known as the author of "Come unto Me" and other serious hymns. He wrote the letters hastily and for the occasion, generally making use of the same subjects he was writing about in editorials.

The difference between the serious editorials and the more effective Nasby letters lay in the inversion of values that the sarcastic approach entailed and the wanton use of propagandistic devices that the approach permitted. Bifurcation was of the essense; the reader was permitted no middle ground. Either he believed the opposite of Nasby or he was damned with him. Nasby dedicated his *Struggles* "To the MAN, Whoever He May Be, Who Succeeds in Bein Elected to the Presidency by the Dimocratic Party, and Who Shall, Immejitly after His Inoggerashun, Appint Me to the Post Offis, from Which the Tyrant Grant Dismist Me, Thus Asurin an Old Dimocrat, Who Never Scratched a Ticket, and Alluz Took His Likker Strate, a Comfortable End to an Uncomfortable Career." Thus the reader was turned against "the MAN" even before he knew who he was.

Personal slander was easy under the guise of Nasby's support. The reader was not permitted to doubt that Andrew Johnson was drunk when he made his infamous "Twenty-second of February" speech in 1866: "I stood beside him," said Nasby. "I helpt hold him up! I SMELT HIS BREATH. It's all rite!"[21] The reader was expected to take Samuel J. Tilden's guilt for granted when Nasby defended him against his Republican "persekooters": "Not content with perventin that gilelis reformer, Saml. J. Tilden, from buyin the Presidency, they are doin their level best to fasten the attempt onto him, and to destroy his chances for another effort in 1880."[22] And one of Nasby's cronies characterized the inventor of the catch phrase "Rum, Romanism, and Rebellion" in the campaign of 1884: "Rev. Burchard made that remark wich helpt us out so gloriously becoz he is a ass ingrane, and coodent help it."[23] In all these instances and many more, David Ross Locke could disclaim responsibility, in a sense, because these were the words of his disreputable characters. Then, too, libel laws were not enforced as they are today. In the mud-slinging campaigns of the Gilded Age, it did not pay to be overscrupulous. If Locke did not help to perpetuate lies, he at least exploited every base rumor that could be used to the advantage of his party. Yet at Locke's funeral, the Reverend Robert McCune, who had known him since he was nineteen, stated: "In all his journalistic career, so far as I know, he never was threatened with a libel suit."[24]

Exaggeration was another of Locke's weapons, and one integral to the sarcastic approach. Though, according to the *Blade,* "there was never any exaggeration in these portraitures,"[25] it is obvious that P. V. Nasby and his friends were representative only of the extremes. Furthermore, Nasby's arguments were generally exaggerated to absurdity. In 1863 he cited "the follerin strictly Dimekratik fact":

> Since the commensement uv the war, the addishn uv niggers to Northern Ohio hez bin ez follows:
>
> | | |
> |---|---|
> | Hancock, | 28,000 |
> | Wood, | 84,000 |
> | Lorane (wich is near Oberlin), | 103,000 |
>
> All uv wich is studyin for the ministry, drawin cavalry captin's pay and rashens, till they gradooate, incloodin two white servants, each.[26]

The entire Negro population of Ohio throughout the war was well below a hundred thousand.

Nasby's lying, exaggeration, and illogicality were well illustrated in his reasons why he should not be drafted:

1. I'm bald-headid, and hev bin obliged to wear a wig these 22 years.

2. I hev dandruff in wat scanty hair still hangs around my venerable temples.

3. I hev kronic katarr.

4. I hev lost, sence Stanton's order to draft, the use uv wun eye entirely, and hev kronic inflammashen in the other.

5. My teeth is all unsound, my palit aint eggsactly rite, and I hev hed bronkeetis 31 yeres last Joon. At present I hev a koff, the paroxisms uv wich is friteful to behold.

6. I'm holler-chestid, am short-winded, and hev alluz hed pains in my back and side.

7. I am afflictid with kronic diarrear and kostivniss. The money I hev paid (or promist to pay), for Jayneses karminnytiv balsam and pills wood astonish almost enny body.

8. I am rupchered in nine places, and am entirely enveloped with trusses.

9. I hev verrykose vanes, hev a white-swellin on wun leg and a fever sore on the uther; also wun leg is shorter than tother, though I handle it so expert that nobody never noticed it.

10. I hev korns and bunyons on both feet, wich wood prevent me from marchin.

I dont suppose that my political opinions, wich are aginst the prossekooshn uv this unconstooshnel war, wood hev any wate with a draftin orfiser; but the above reasons why I cant go, will, I make no doubt, be suffishent.[27]

Like some of his comic contemporaries, Nasby was somewhat adept at misquoting. After Shakespeare, he told us that he was in "the sere and yeller leef," and he referred to the "tented fields" of the war. Other writers were less frequently alluded to. As a Democratic office-holder, Nasby echoed Bryant in his advice to fellow appointees: "Let us go slow, draw our salaries to the end uv our 'spective terms, and so live that wen the summons comes to jine the innoomerable caravan that moves out uv Washinton to'ards their 'spective homes, we go not like the dusty slave at nite, wat's bet his all on two pair, but soothed and sustained by wat we saved,—go like one who's got the wherewithal to live."[28]

It was the Bible, however, that Nasby was most familiar with. His favorite passages were those upon which he based his arguments for Negro slavery: Genesis 9:20-27, Noah's curse on the children of Ham; and Paul's Epistle to Philemon, which involves the return of a servant to his master. Nasby interpreted Noah's curse as follows:

> Noah, after the water went down, come down from Aryrat, went into farmin, and planted grapes extensive. One day he took a drink too much, and laid down with insuffishent clothin onto him. His second son, Ham, saw him in that fix, and when Noah awoke, while his hair wuz still pullin, he cust him and his posterity, and sed they shood be servants forever.
>
> Ham (wich in the original Hebrew signifies the hind-quarter uv a hog), wuz the father uv the Afrikins, and they hev bin slaves ever sence.
>
> I seed a lite to-wunst—I realized the importance uv the nigger. He is the connectin link in the chain uv circumstances wich led to the formashen uv the Dimekratic party. He hez kept the blessid old macheen a runnin to this day. Observe:
>
> Whisky (or wine, wich is the same thing) made Noah tight.
> Ham saw Noah inebriated.
> Noah cust Ham, wich turned him into a nigger and a servant.
> That the Skripters mite be fulfilled, the children uv Ham wuz brot to America, to be servants here.
> Wickid men set themselves agin the Skripters, and tried to make men uv the niggers.
> The Dimekratik party ariz for the purpus uv keepin the nigger down, and that deliteful biznis hez given them employment for more than 30 years. . . .
> Whisky! Nigger! Dimokrasy! O, savory trinity!
> We don't none uv us read the Skripters enuff.[29]

The Reverend Nasby quoted, paraphrased, burlesqued, and alluded to the Bible frequently. Part of the purpose here was merely the incongruity between the sober style of the King

James translation and the ridiculous message of Nasby. But a more important purpose was the blasphemy of Nasby's use of the Bible—a sin to be associated with the party he represented. Thus did Locke use every trick he could devise to vilify the opposition.

Nor did he stop within the limits of respectable taste. Unconcerned with posterity or with the genteel reading public, he wrote the Nasby letters for rough Midwestern farmers—the readers of the *Hancock Jeffersonian* and the *Weekly Blade*—and he made sure that what he wrote was strong enough to move them. Racy figures of speech were not uncommon, as when Nasby described his state of jubilation over election results as feeling like "a bridegroom, wich cometh from his bride in the mornin feelin releeved in the knowledge that she wore not palpitators, nor false calves, nor nothin false, afore she wuz hizn."[30] His references to miscegenation and adultery on Southern plantations were pointed and bald. The Nasby letter of April 20, 1865, on the assassination of Lincoln is still, perhaps, to be considered in bad taste. The hypocritical Nasby pretended to mourn the event, but his worst feelings showed through: "Hed it happened in 1862, when it wood hev been uv sum use to us, we wood not be so bowed down with woe and anguish." And, as late as 1880, Locke was waving the bloody shirt in the most horrendous manner when he described a Democratic meeting at Confedrit X Roads:

> The meetin-house hed bin dekoratid by the patriotic wimmin uv the Corners in the most gorgeous stile. The two candlesticks on the pulpit wuz furnished by Miss Melindy Pogram, bein made from the thigh-bones uv Fedrel hirelins wich perished, justly, at Andersonville; the hammer yoosed by the cheerman wuz the shin bone uv a nigger wich went up at Fort Piller, and the Confedrit flag wuz tastefully draped over portrates uv Ginral Lee, Jefferson Davis and other heroes, who gave theirselves to the coz uv the sunny (now solid) South.[31]

Locke may be compared to Jonathan Swift in the extremity of his means for persuasive effect. He is reminiscent of Swift in his description of the burning of a Negro schoolhouse: "The cry uv the nigger children wich coodent escape, symbolized their desertid condishn, and the smell uv em, ez they roasted, wuz like unto incense, grateful to our nostrils."[32]

V *Achievement*

Locke's techniques in the Nasby papers were obvious and coarse. But he was welcomed by Northern leaders because he was undoubtedly effective. That was his aim and he was pre-eminently successful in it. Except for Benjamin Franklin, he stands alone in American letters as a satiric propagandist. Like Harriet Beecher Stowe, Locke presented one side of the argument with such powerful simplicity that it could not be ignored. Like Thomas Paine, he was unfailingly ready at the psychological moment with words that told. Lincoln's Secretary of the Treasury George S. Boutwell attributed the defeat of the South in the Civil War to three forces: the Army, the Navy, and the Nasby letters.

As pure literature, the Nasby letters had their faults. They were verbose, hasty, repetitious, inconsistent. Their spelling and their timely allusions make them formidable reading today. And their truth was always slanted.

Yet their impact can only be explained on literary grounds. There was plenty of journalism in Locke's time that handled the same subject matter, but none that was remembered then or now with the same clarity. Adopting the conventions of the crackerbox humorists and speaking from the supposed point of view of the opposition, Locke exposed the falsities of its position and ridiculed its presumptions. The hyperbole, the stacking of the evidence, the racy metaphors were deliberate political weapons.

As part of the culture of their time, the Nasby letters illustrate its strong and biased journalism; its political heat; its class, race, and nationality prejudices; and its regional antipathies. Written for the recently literate mass audience, they reflect the pervasion of politics into all segments of American life and the sensational-ism induced by political strife. They could only have been written in America and only during the periods of the threatened disunion of the Civil War and the political and social immorality of the Gilded Age.

The Nasby letters are a vitally partisan chronicle of a crucial quarter century of American history. They are detailed and comprehensive, yet uninhibited by any attempt to show two sides to every issue. Though unreliable as factual history, they exhibit what might be termed the psychological history of Republicanism from Lincoln to Blaine. Their violence reflects the underlying violence of the society from which they sprang, and no unimpassioned survey of the period can equal them.

CHAPTER *4*

Belles Lettres

D AVID ROSS LOCKE'S amazing versatility showed itself
in the variety of genres he attempted, with a considerable
degree of success in each. Besides editorial, news, and feature
writing; occasional magazine articles; and the Nasby letters, he
produced a book of travels, a series of mock-oriental tales, a
narrative in verse, several hymns, two plays, three formal lectures
as well as other speeches, and a vast amount of newspaper
fiction. In all his work he demonstrated homely wit, worldly
sagacity, and a remarkable fluency of rhetoric. His themes were
generally the glorification of the practical American and the
criticism of social evils. His posture was that of a practical
moralist; and, though his moral views were seldom new or
radical, he supported most of the reforms of his age and gave
more than mere sympathy to the downtrodden. He tried too
much, of course, and because of the great quantity of his produc-
tion, he fell short of the first rank in all his literary roles except
that of political satirist. Locke wrote and published over a
million words in addition to his several columns per week of
regular newspaper writing during his lifetime. It is remarkable
then that he achieved what he did in quality. His work remains
as representative, not of the best but of the good writing
of his time.

I Nasby in Exile

Locke's travel book, *Nasby in Exile* (1882), naturally invites
comparison with Mark Twain's *Innocents Abroad* (1869). Both
books presented the practical American's skepticism toward
European values. Both ridiculed the monarchical system and

praised democracy. Both minimized the masterpieces of European culture and concentrated on human interest. Locke said in his Preface:

> The only difference between this book and the thousands of others that have been printed describing the same scenes, is purely the difference in the eyes of the writers who saw them. I saw the countries I visited with a pair of American eyes, and judged of men and things from a purely American stand-point. . . . I was interested in the men and women of the countries I passed through, I was interested in their ways of living, their industries and their customs and habits, and I tried faithfully to put upon paper what I saw, as well as the observations and comments of the party that traveled and observed with me.[1]

Locke's book was far less comic than Twain's. Though *Nasby in Exile* abounded in humor, the author's purpose was primarily to share his experience with his reader. Despite the title, the book had nothing to do with the Petroleum V. Nasby of Confedrit X Roads. The narrator was essentially David Ross Locke, who posed as a genial, sedentary American on a vacation, although the comic illustrations by R. Lorenz pictured him with the customary features of the old reprobate, who had been most effectively drawn by Thomas Nast. There was no dialect or bad spelling, and the narrator had the reader's good will.

Locke had contemplated a series entitled "Nasby in Eggsile," and he actually wrote five letters from July to November, 1881, in the style of Petroleum V. Nasby. Those letters, published in *The Nasby Letters* after Locke's death, violently satirized the Irish Republican movement, and they were abruptly broken off at about the time Locke visited Ireland and reversed his view. They were in marked contrast to the genial approach of *Nasby in Exile*.

Meanwhile, *Nasby in Exile*, published serially in the *Blade*, honestly reflected Locke's newly acquired wisdom:

> Irish landlordism is condensed villainy. It is the very top and summit of oppression, cruelty, brutality and terror.
> It is conceived in lust and greed, born of fraud, and perpetuated by force.

It does not recognize manhood, womanhood or childhood. Its cold hand is upon every cradle in Ireland. Its victims are the five millions of people in Ireland who cannot get away, and the instruments used to hold them are bayonets and ball cartridges.[2]

Four of the book's forty-five chapters were devoted to the plight of the Irish, and the subject threatened to take the place of the earlier Negro problem in Locke's mind. The other chapters, however, dealt with the incidents of travel in England, France, Switzerland, and Germany. Besides "Nasby," the party consisted of the young man Lemuel Tibbitts, the pedantic Professor, and the *nouveau-riche* faro banker's wife—all of whom served to call forth observations and to provide comic relief.

Tibbitts was especially entertaining. He wrote gushing letters to his mother in Oshkosh, Wisconsin, about the sights he generally failed to see because of his preference for drinking and night life. His adventures with Swiss guides were right out of *Innocents Abroad:*

In every country in the world that has rocks, there is some frightfully high one from which a great many years ago a maiden leaped. Indian maidens were addicted to this in America, and so were maidens in Switzerland. . . .

Tibbitts looked calmly down the frightful chasm.

"The maiden leaped from this spot?"

"Yes, sare."

"How under Heaven did she *ever* get back!"

"She did not get back."

"Did she hurt herself?"

"Hurt hairselluf! It ees five huntret veet to ze bottom. How could she fall five huntret veet and not hurt hairselluf?"

"Five hundred feet! Well, I should say it was rather risky. What did the old folks do about it?"

He wanted to know all the circumstances, but the information of guides on such subjects always ends with the bloodcurdling tragedy. They know nothing of what happened after the girl took the fatal plunge.[3]

And Tibbitts continually embarrassed the Professor by his cynical views of treasured antiquities.

The gambler's wife typified American vulgarity. She learned

nothing whatever from her surroundings, and she was concerned only with her appearance:

> Foreign travel is of a vast amount of use to a great many people. Coming from Dieppe to Paris there were seated in our compartment two ladies with their husbands, who were in New York, bankers, one regular and the other faro, and both with loads of money. The wife of the faro banker was arrayed in the most gorgeous and fearfully expensive apparel, with a No. 6 foot in a No. 4 shoe. The other lady *was* a lady, and she really desired to see something of the country she was traveling through. The faro bankeress talked to her from Dieppe to St. Lazarre station, and this was about what she said:—
>
> "You never saw anything so perfectly lovely as the children's ball last year at the Academy of Music. My little girl, Lulu, you saw her at the school—she goes to the same school with your Minnie, only Lulu isn't studying anything but French and geography now. I want her to get to be perfect in French, because it will be such a comfort to travel with her, and see things, and not be entirely dependent upon your maid—we have a maid with us, but, of course, we have her travel third-class—not for the difference in the expense, for we don't have to economize—but you know it won't do to have your servants too close to you; they get to presuming upon their privileges, and you must make them know their place. Oh, I wish we had a monarchy or something of the kind in America, so that we could be divided up into classes, and not be compelled to mix with the lower orders. . . ."
>
> "Oh heavens! do look at that beautiful valley," exclaimed the unwilling listener.
>
> There was a valley spread out before us, so entirely perfect in its soft loveliness that it was worth a voyage across the Atlantic to see it. The faro bankeress glanced out of the window, and with the remark, "It's altogether too lovely for anything," went on without a moment's pause:—
>
> "I had a dress made of a white material that represented ice, with little balls of white down to represent snow balls all over it, and furs, the edges trimmed with down. . . ."[4]

In addition to this cast of characters, the narrator met an American circus manager scouting for "attractions," several poor Irish families, Jewish traders, and German students, as well as numerous guides, barkeepers, and hotel managers. He visited not only the Tower of London, the Castle of Chillon, and the Heidelberg Tun, but the pubs of London and the cafés of Paris, the ghettos of London and Frankfort, the Irish bogs and the Swiss workshops. He interspersed European legends with American anecdotes. And although there were occasional purple passages of scenic description, probably written by Robinson Locke who accompanied his father throughout the tour, they were rare enough not to be burdensome, and the general style was one of colloquial ease and genial amusement.

A fine example of amusing and fairly informative travel literature, *Nasby in Exile* was also a valid contribution to the international theme—the meeting of the Old World and the New. Though Locke was not the sensitive observer of a Henry James novel, nor quite the bumptious critic of Mark Twain's pose, he was an intelligent reporter and a representative American recording typical impressions. He saw things pretty much as they were, with always a democratic sympathy for the laborer; he seldom sentimentalized and he showed a healthy disdain for the frills and ills of aristocracy and for the romanticizing of the "Culture" lover.

II The Morals of Abou Ben Adhem

In *The Morals of Abou Ben Adhem* or *Eastern Fruit in Western Dishes* (1875), Locke approached his public in yet another guise. Capitalizing on the popularity of Oriental and pseudo-Oriental wisdom, he adopted the name of Leigh Hunt's lover of mankind to present American horse sense in a new way. Locke's Abou turned out to be an imposter, one Zephaniah Scudder of Maine. Instead of a Persian sage, possessor of the secrets of eternal youth and of the transmutation of metals, "he had taught dancing, singing, writing; he had been a horse-tamer, a veterinary surgeon, a dentist, a showman, a politician, an editor in a small way; he had preached, practised medicine, speculated in lands, and in everything else; he had married wives in a dozen places; in short, he had done everything that was disreputable or semi-disreputable, and had finally embarked

[103]

in counterfeiting the smallest coin, but two, that our Government makes."⁵ Yet his philosophy was generally sound and illustrated the truism that advice may be good though the adviser is not. "Chin-music is cheaper even than that of the hand-organ," said Abou. "Doth advice cost? Go to!"⁶

Locke had used the character of Abou Ben Adhem in the story of "The Diskontentid Pezant. A Orientale Allegory, with a Moral onto It," told in the words of P. V. Nasby and printed in *Divers Views, Opinions, and Prophecies* in 1866. The story was rewritten and enlarged for publication in *Locke's National Monthly* in March, 1873, where the Abou Ben Adhem stories first appeared as a series. It told of a young man who begged Abou to make his sheep produce wool already carded into rolls, so as to save him the labor of carding. The sage granted his request, but the youth reappeared a week later to ask that the wool might grow already spun into yarn. Still not satisfied with the granting of the second request, the youth returned to ask for whole cloth from his sheep. Upon his fourth appearance, he asked:

"Why stop at cloth? Why, O Abou, should they not grow——"
"What?" shrieked Abou, bewildered at the young man's impudence.
The young man was not bewildered, or dashed, or in any way moved. He was as calm as a summer's morning. Taking Abou by the button-hole that he might not escape him, he fixed him with his eye, and proceeded,——
"Why should they not as well grow ready-made clothing, with an American watch in the vest-pocket? This is what I now want. Grant me this, and be chesm, I swear by Bismallah——"
"Away, ungrateful dog, and let me see thy face no more!" shrieked the indignant Abou, his eyes glowing fiercely, like the head-light of a locomotive. "Three times have I granted thy absurd wishes knowing full well that it would come to this. I yielded to thy importunities solely and entirely for the purpose of teaching thee a lesson,—one that every young man must learn before he can be happy.
"Nature, wretched man, did for us, at the beginning, all that was needed,—all that our imperfect being could endure. She gave us the raw material to work on, and the ability to work on

it, and then very properly let us alone. She gave us stomachs, but did not stop there. She gave us cattle, and wheat, and things of that character. I suppose she could have put up cattle ready roasted; she might have had sirloin roasts on four legs rambling pensively on the hills, waiting to be eaten; and each stalk of wheat might have had a French roll on its head, and so on: but she knew better than that. It is our business to utilize her gifts. Nature provides corn: it is for us to convert that corn into bread and such other products as go to sustain life.

"Suppose, O miserable! for instance, that I had given you all you asked: what would you have had to do, and how would you have done it? You would have become lazy and worthless; you would have frequented groceries; you would have intensified your taste for intoxicating beverages; to kill time you would have resorted to faro and keno, two sinful games that will floor a man quicker than anything in this world, as I know ever since I made the last trip to Trenton, where I lost—but no matter; you would have mixed in politics and become a nuisance to yourself and a pest to your friends."[7]

Of the twenty-eight fables in *The Morals of Abou Ben Adhem*, three others were originally told by Nasby in *Divers Views* and were rewritten to fit the burlesque-Oriental style of the book. One of these appeared in three versions: Nasby's "Indulges in a Reminiscence of His Youthful Days," 1866; a straight version, "The Misanthrope," in *Locke's National Monthly*, December, 1872; and an Oriental version, "The Faithlessness of Woman," in the book of 1875. Thus Locke economized—in his busy career—by reusing earlier ideas.

"The Faithlessness of Woman" was the story of two suitors of the same girl, who, having been sent by her to make their fortunes, returned to find her married to a third. Abou, for he was one of the wronged suitors in the final version of the story, related his reaction:

I was despondent for an age,—that is, for four days. But by degrees the aspect of things changed. I concluded that I would not die, but that I would live, and work my way to such a height of grandeur that Zara would never cease to regret that she jilted me. In two weeks I found myself totally indifferent to her, and in a month I was rejoiced that I had escaped her; for her husband discovered that she had a tongue, and to use an Orientalism, she made it warm for him.[8]

The story was reminiscent of Oliver Goldsmith's *The Citizen of the World,* as indeed the whole book was; and there was, in fact, a deliberate reference to Goldsmith on the third page of the Introduction. Locke's book was generally good-natured satire of human nature and contemporary society. He commented—like Goldsmith—on loyalty, honesty, fame, and fear of death; and he lightly ridiculed fashions in clothing, money-getting, and courtship and marriage. But in making his philosopher a rogue, Locke avoided a sententious tone and poked fun at the solemnity of pseudo-religious moralizing. The reader was permitted to take Abou's morals just as seriously as he wished, but they were not forced down his throat.

On rare occasion, Locke's own basic seriousness came to the fore in *The Morals of Abou Ben Adhem,* and his satire turned bitter. In "The Utility of Death," he became personal: "And then think of a world with such pests as George Francis Train and the [Victoria Claflin] Woodhull in it, with no prospect of relief from Death?"[9] But on the whole, his humor was at its sprightliest in this book. Written for his monthly magazine, as most of these stories were, the sayings of Abou were meant for a more refined audience than was most of Locke's writing. They thus lacked the personal bitterness and the exclusively timely subjects of the Nasby letters, and are quite readable—though unread—today. *The Morals of Abou Ben Adhem* was Locke's most humorous writing.

III *Verse*

In approaching Locke's poetry—as approach it we must—we need to keep in mind his remarkable achievements in other fields and we can perhaps forgive him for "slopping over." His most famous poem was *Hannah Jane,* published in red and gold binding by Lee and Shepard in Boston and Charles T. Dillingham in New York in 1882, printed in rich format by University Press:

John Wilson & Son, Cambridge, and lushly illustrated by S. G. McCutcheon and E. H. Garrett. On lecture tours, it became a custom for Locke's audiences to applaud, at the conclusion of the speech, until they should be treated with a reading of *Hannah Jane*.

Hannah Jane was a symptom of the times. It was also, perhaps, an expiatory tribute to Locke's wife, whose middle name was Hannah. And finally, it reflected the author's concern for woman's lot in nineteenth-century civilization. In twenty-nine, four-line stanzas of iambic heptameter couplets, the first-person narrator told of the wife who remained true through hardship and neglect. The final stanza will suffice to show the mixture of mawkish sentiment and bungling jargon:

> There's another world beyond this; and on the final day
> Will intellect and learning against such devotion weigh?
> And when the one made of us two, is torn apart again,
> I'll kick the beam, for God is just, and He knows Hannah Jane.

Locke probably wrote a number of "poems," both serious and comic, in the columns of his newspapers without signing them; but, aside from the humorous doggerel reprinted in *Divers Views, Opinions, and Prophecies of Petroleum V. Nasby,* his only verse of any significance was his hymns. With a limited understanding of music, he could appreciate and love Protestant hymns. His deep-seated religiousness was best expressed by a full-toned hymn, whether he heard it sung or bellowed it forth himself.

He wrote the words to at least five hymns, at least two of which were set to music. The five—"Come unto Me," "Thou Son of David Have Mercy on Me," "Let Me But Touch His Garment," "Oh, Lord, Make Haste to Help Me!" "Light, Faith, Strength"— were published in the *Weekly Blade* in the weeks following his death. "Come unto Me," probably the best known, was sung at Locke's funeral. All of them showed a mastery of the polished, artificial poetic diction characteristic of the genteel age. The pungency of Locke's prose was all polished out of his verse. Yet there remained a glimmering of sincerity that made the hymns a little better than mere competent exercises in a conventional form. "Oh, Lord, Make Haste to Help Me!" was the best example. It was based on Psalms 40:12-13:

> There is a purer air than this which clings
>   About me here, in these foul lower skies;
> I fain would reach it, but my spirit's wings
>   Are weak and nerveless, and I cannot rise.
> The greed of earth, and soul-destroying care,
> Hold me below, in sin-infested air.
>
> There is a stream whose living waters flow
>   Straight from the throne, and whoso bathes therein,
> The cruel pangs of death shall never know,
>   But ransomed be from the fell power of sin.
> I strive in vain; I fall, too weak to rise,
> The glittering water shining in my eyes.
>
> There is a land where 'tis eternal day,
>   And souls forever bask in purest light.
> My purblind vision sees all clear the way,
>   I struggle to'ard it with my feeble might,
> My feet are earth-held, and all strength I lack,
> The weakening lusts of earth all hold me back.
>
> Jesus! sweet Savior! the strong wings art thou,
>   And thou the strength my longing soul doth crave;
> Humble and helpless at thy feet I bow,
>   For thou, and thou alone, hast power to save.
> Oh, turn on a lost soul thy pitying face,
> Bowed down and broken, I do trust thy grace.

One can hardly miss the autobiographical implications of these lines. A strong sense of guilt pervaded Locke's life. Though he grew up under the influence of Methodism, the God of his hymns was a Puritan God. Depraved man was saved from a well-deserved hell only by the grace of God, symbolized by Jesus. Stern justice would condemn most—probably all—men; the only hope was God's mercy. The "sin-infested air" of the world was gloomy and bitter. The glimmering vision of ever-lasting life was in sharp contrast. The lost soul could only pray that Christ would turn on him His "pitying face." Through the somewhat hackneyed imagery of the hymn, the reader can sense the hopes and fears of David Ross Locke as he viewed approaching death.

Locke seemed to consider his hymns his most serious work, and hoped that they, if anything, would live. They are not to be found, however, in any of the standard collections or listings of American hymnology.

IV *Drama*

No copy of either of Locke's plays has been found. A discussion of Locke as a dramatist must necessarily be based on the accounts of those who saw the plays. Both *Inflation* (1876), by Locke and Charles Gayler, and *Widow Bedott* (1879), based by Locke on the writings of Frances Whitcher, were registered in the United States Copyright Office before their first performance, but copies were not deposited.

Inflation, or *The Xs of the X Roads,* was probably a dramatized version of Locke's pamphlet *Inflation at the Cross Roads* (1875), which in turn was composed of the Nasby letters from the *Blade* that were written in opposition to the paper money movement. If so, the topical nature of the material, the repulsive character of Nasby and his associates, and the brutality of some of the action may have offended the nineteenth-century sense of propriety; for there is no evidence that the play was performed more than once. Perhaps it is true that there are scenes fit to be read that are not fit for the stage. The unalleviated barroom brawls, riots, and lynching mobs of this series of Nasby letters may not be good theater. Then, too, the real subject of the letters is a lesson in economics, a subject that may be undramatic per se. A revealing impression of the play was recorded in the diary of James A. Garfield, who classed it with the dramatized version of Mark Twain's and Charles Dudley Warner's *The Gilded Age:* "It is one of the cheap and extravagant specimens of literature which I think will fail as it certainly ought to. The play is based on the assumed universal corruption of public men presented in the baldest and most absurd form. The piece was written by D. R. Locke and indicates how low down he must have fallen as a thinker."[10] It would nonetheless be interesting to see *Inflation* performed on the twentieth-century stage—if it could be found.

Widow Bedott, or *A Hunt for a Husband,* was not topical at all; and it contained none of the hard-hitting satire of the Nasby letters. It was one of the solid successes of the late nineteenth-century stage. According to the New York *Mirror,* Locke did not attempt to follow Mrs. Whitcher's lines exactly but flawlessly reproduced the spirit of the original *The Widow Bedott Papers:* "Little of the dialogue is taken directly from the papers, and when, for dramatic purposes, interpolation or alteration was necessary, the style has been imitated so exactly that the closest scrutiny is necessary to detect where the original left off and the dramatist begun. The scheming Widow and the simple-minded Elder are presented precisely as they were created, in every particular, voice, costume, and expression."

As background to the character of the widow, Locke added a conventional plot. The romance between the officious widow and the pious Elder Sniffles was balanced by the search for a husband for the widow's daughter. Farcical confusions as to who was pursuing whom, and the revelation that most of the characters were more interested in a rich settlement than in romantic love, constituted the main action. The real interest in the play lay in the characterization of the widow. The Providence, Rhode Island, *Journal* said:

> It will be seen by this that the plot is not complicated or difficult, and the strength of the play is in its characters and the felicity of its dialogue. The two principal characters are very complete, drawn with a firm hand and as distinct as Nasby himself or any of the personages of the Confederate X Roads. They are extreme types, both actual and living ones, not mere bundles of extravagances, and both consistent and realistic. They are, to a certain extent, caricatures, but especially mark the difference between caricature and extravagance in the deepening of the natural effect, and intensifying rather than destroying it. They are such caricatures as may be seen in Hogarth's "Morning," and in other of his plates, exaggerated but vivid and perfect in

themselves. The dialogue is full of a broad humor and very felicitous strokes, whose point is not to be missed. The widow's expression, "I believe in election and damnation—election for myself and damnation for most other people—and I take great comfort in it," is a fair though not the brightest specimen, and the humor is as abundant as it is unctuous and amusing. It is not the genteel comedy, such as flourished before Goldsmith, nor resembles the thin and highly polished dramas of Robertson and Byron in the present day. In the technical term it would be called low comedy, and perhaps, but for its length, denominated a farce; but it is a very amusing and successful play under whatever title it may be called.[11]

According to the *Mirror*, Locke had written the play in 1869, but had laid it aside until he happened to see Neil Burgess, whose skill at female impersonation made him a natural for the leading role. Burgess made an immediate and triumphant success of the widow. "He was not the least bit effeminate ... and yet he was the Widow Bedott to the life, and with little exaggeration of burlesque."[12] After the first performance in Providence, the author and the actor carefully reworked the play, cutting the long speeches, brightening the dialogue, and sharpening the characterization, so that the excessive length of the first performance was remedied when the play appeared in New York City. Admitting its stage success, the reviewers were nonetheless skeptical of its literary merit, despite the pains of the author and the actor. The *Mirror* said: "Mr. Locke invites no attention to his youngling on the score of literary worth or dramatic merit. It contains neither. But it is excessively funny." And the New York *Times*: "The farce of 'Widow Bedott,' which is a better play than most of its kind, is as coarse and grossly exaggerated as the once popular book upon which it is founded, but when Mr. Burgess is on the stage the fun never flags."[13]

V *Lecture*

As a lecturer Locke achieved his most polished success. The finished effect of his three published lectures, and the mere fact that he had to present each of them before live audiences hundreds of times, suggest that he took more pains in writing them than with any of his other work, with the possible exception of some of his verse. His self-respect as a lecturer was attested by his friend and fellow-lecturer Mark Twain. His effectiveness depended entirely on his reputation and the preparation of his manuscript, for he had little natural ability as a speaker and made no apparent effort to learn. Indeed, his bull-headed artlessness on the platform seems to have had a certain attractiveness in itself. Twain described his performance:

> His appearance on the stage was welcomed with a prodigious burst of applause, but he did not stop to bow or in any other way acknowledge the greeting, but strode straight to the reading desk, spread his portfolio open upon it, and immediately petrified himself into an attitude which he never changed during the hour and a half occupied by his performance, except to turn his leaves—his body bent over the desk, rigidly supported by his left arm, as by a stake, the right arm lying across his back. About once in two minutes his right arm swung forward, turned a leaf, then swung to its resting-place on his back again—just the action of a machine, and suggestive of one; regular, recurrent, prompt, exact. You might imagine you heard it *clash*. He was a great, burly figure, uncouthly and provincially clothed, and he looked like a simple old farmer.
>
> I was all curiosity to hear him begin. He did not keep me waiting. The moment he had crutched himself upon his left arm, lodged his right upon his back, and bent himself over his manuscript he raised his face slightly, flashed a glance upon the audience, and bellowed this remark in a thundering bull-voice:
>
> *"We are all descended from grandfathers!"*
>
> Then he went right on roaring to the end, tearing his ruthless way through the continuous applause and laughter, and taking no sort of account of it. His lecture was a volleying and sustained discharge of bull's-eye hits, with the slave power and its Northern apologists for target, and his success was due to his matter, not his manner; for his delivery was destitute of art, unless a tremendous and inspiring earnestness and energy may be called by that name. The moment he had finished his piece he turned his back and marched off the stage with the seeming of being not personally concerned with the applause that was booming behind him.[14]

Though Locke is often classed with Artemus Ward, Josh Billings, and Mark Twain as a comic lecturer, he did not really belong to the tradition originated by Artemus nor did he have anything in common with them. Their lectures were never read; Locke's eyes were glued to his manuscript. Their art depended on complete rapport with the audience; Locke had none. They developed an apparently casual, unconscious style that depended on subtle timing, careful anticlimax, and deliberate stumbling; Locke proceeded from beginning to end without pause or expression. They were most immediately concerned with getting a laugh; Locke seemed not even to notice it. Consequently, the content of their lectures was often shallow; Locke's was both serious and important.

Locke's lectures were much more closely related to his own Nasby papers than to the lectures of any of his fellows. Although he did enjoy popular favor by being categorized with them, he used his own original approach. He always billed himself as Petroleum V. Nasby, and in "Cussid Be Canaan" he posed as Nasby, but with modifications. He did not use the substandard language nor did he dress in the outlandish costume associated with his literary creation. But he did—in all three printed lectures—pose as a defender of the wrong; and, by the same methods he used in the Nasby letters, he exposed the falsity of that position. Again, there was little humor in his presentation: his chief weapon was sarcasm.

In the lecture, it was necessary to make clear from the beginning that the pose was a pose; he could not have his audience feeling toward him the contempt they were supposed to feel toward Nasby. He began "Cussid Be Canaan" by introducing a line from the Declaration of Independence, and then clearly delineating the mock position that he was going to take:

> Thomas Jefferson was the particular grandfather who wrote those high-sounding words, and, as a consequence, he has been ever since hailed as the father of the only political party which never believed in them. My particular mission is to show that Jefferson was a most shallow person, which opinion of Jefferson is very general in the South. True, the Democracy claim him

as its father: but when we remember that the same party claim Jackson, the strangler of secession, as another father, we can easily see how that can be. We have claimed these men as ancestors only since they departed this life.[15]

Next he revised Jefferson's words, and made it clear that he was speaking as Nasby by a reference to Nasby's town, Confedrit X Roads, which was already well known to his audience:

"We hold these *supposed* truths to be *tolerably* self-evident, that, as a rule, all *white* men are created equal; that *they* are endowed by their Creator with divers and sundry rights, which may be considered inalienable: that among these are life, liberty, and the pursuit of——niggers!"

It will be observed that the two Declarations differ somewhat. One is as Jefferson wrote it, and the other is the version we use at Confedrit X Roads.[16]

After further ridiculing the racist position by suggesting the revision of all great literature on such lines as "Breathes there a white male, with soul so dead," Nasby proceeded to expound his reasons for believing the Negro to be damned by God to perpetual slavery and to be not a man at all, but a beast. Each reason was put in such a grotesque light that it was impossible for any sane person to agree. The exposition continued with a historical survey of the Negroes' position and concluded with a depiction of the Democrats' curtailing of Negroes' rights and of the Republicans' cowardice in not enforcing those rights:

The Republican party was brave enough to face the armies of the rebellion, but it was not brave enough to face a prejudice. From the close of the war up to this winter, in the very flush of the victories they had won by the aid of the strong hands of their black allies, they coolly betrayed them. So magnanimous were they, so generous were they to their enemies, that they forgot their friends. They gave us, their late masters, the right to disfranchise them at any time. They gave Southern legislatures the power to reduce them again to serfdom, and even those in the Northern States were denied their rights.[17]

The concluding section of the lecture was a complete reversal of the Nasby pose. Here Locke spoke, in complete seriousness and stirring rhetoric. The shift was clearly marked:

How shall we dispose of the negro. He was ever a disturbing element in American politics, and ever will be so long as left in the position he has occupied. The curse theory is worthless, and the beast theory leaks like a sieve. If there ever was anything in the curse it has all faded out, and if he is not a man, he is a most excellent imitation. We have abandoned the Nasbyan theory, and have fallen back upon Jefferson. Now that the government is in a transition state, now that we can make of it what we will, suppose that we rebuild upon a safe and sure foundation.[18]

The needed foundation was guaranteed suffrage and equal rights. The lecture ended with a resounding flourish that brought the listener back to the Declaration:

Casting behind us, as unworthy of a moment's serious consideration, the miserable sophistries of the false teachers who have well nigh ruined the republic, let us dare to do right. Let us declare and crystalize our Declaration into unchangeable laws, that under the flag all men shall be men. Let us build an altar, the foundation of which shall be Reason, the topstone Justice, and laying thereon our prejudices, let them be consumed in the steady, pure flame of Humanity. The smell of that sacrifice will be a sweeter savor to the Father of all races than any since Abel's. Let us raise ourselves from the low, dead, flat plane of self-interest, and demonstrate our strength, not by trampling upon the defenceless heads of those weaker and lower than ourselves, but by lifting them up to us. And then, when the flag has under its shadow only free men, when all men are recognized as men, we can look the world in the face, and repeat without a blush that grand old Declaration, that Magna Charta of human rights, that Evangel of Humanity: "We hold these truths to be self-evident, that all men are created equal; that they are endowed by their Creator with certain inalienable rights; that among these are life, liberty, and the pursuit of happiness."[19]

The ratification of the Fifteenth Amendment in 1870 was the achievement for which Locke had been fighting. Or so he felt at the time, at least. "Cussid Be Canaan" was his most comprehensive statement of his convictions on the Negro question. His next lecture, "The Struggles of a Conservative with the Woman Question," was his strongest stand on female suffrage, and "In Search of the Man of Sin" comprehended his whole attitude toward evil in human society. All three lectures were developed on the same plan: the clarification of the pose, the exposition of the arguments, and the serious reversal. Although Locke continued to be billed as Nasby, he gave up all attempts to pose as the sage of Confedrit X Roads in his second lecture; and he pretended in "In Search of the Man of Sin" to have been born in Maine and to be residing in Vermont. Yet in all three lectures, the pose was transparently antagonistic and the method was to reduce the opposition's arguments to absurdity.

"The Struggles of a Conservative" was an outright demand for woman suffrage. It began with an explanation of the conservative: "I grew up with reverence for everything old. I am not the man who caught hold of the coat-tail of Progress, and yelled 'Whoa!' I do not believe there ever was such a man. Progress does not wear a coat: he rushes by in his shirt sleeves; and, besides, your true Conservative, of whom I am which, never gets awake in time to see Progress whistle by."[20]

The conservative's attitude toward women was introduced in a fine paragraph "in praise of" woman, which anticipated Mark Twain's famous toast to the ladies, and very possibly was Twain's source of inspiration:

> I adore woman. I recognize the importance of the sex, and lay at its feet my humble tribute. But for woman, where would we have been? Who in our infancy washed our faces, fed us soothing syrup, and taught us "How doth the little busy bee?" Woman! To whom did we give red apples in our boyhood? *for whom* did we part our hair behind, and wear No. 7 boots when No. 10's would have been more comfortable? and WITH WHOM did we sit up nights, in the hair-oil period of our existence?

And finally, whom did we marry? But for woman what would the novelists have done? What would have become of Sylvanus Cobb, Jr., if he had had no women to make heroines of? And without Sylvanus Cobb, Bonner could not have made the Ledger a success; Everett would be remembered not as the man who wrote for the Ledger, but merely as an orator and statesman; Beecher never would have written Norwood, and Dexter might to-day have been chafing under the collar in a dray! But for woman George Washington would not have been the father of his country, the Sunday school teachers would have been short the affecting story of the little hatchet and the cherry tree, and half the babies in the country would have been named after some one else. Possibly they might have all been Smiths. But for woman Andrew Johnson never would have been, and future generations would have lost the most awful example of depravity the world has ever seen. I adore woman, but I want her to keep her place. I don't want woman to be the coming man![21]

At the end of the lecture came the reversal, and Locke's real views were directly stated:

I have tried for an hour to be a conservative, but it won't do. Like poor calico, it won't wash. There are in the United States some millions of women who desire something better than the lives they and their mothers have been living. There are millions of women who have minds and souls, and who yearn for something to develop their minds and souls. There are millions of women who desire to have something to think about, to assume responsibilities, that they may strengthen their moral natures, as the gymnast lifts weights to strengthen his physical nature. There are hundreds of thousands of women who have suffered in silence worse evils by far than the slaves of the South, who, like the slaves of the South, have no power to redress their wrongs, no voice so potent that the public must hear. In the parlor, inanity and frivolity: in the cottage, hopeless servitude, unceasing toil; a dark life, with a darker ending. This is the condition of woman in the world to-day. Thousands starving physically for want of something to do, with a world calling for labor; thousands starving mentally, with an unexplored world before them. One half of humanity is a burden on the other half.[22]

"In Search of the Man of Sin" used the same strategy as that of the other lectures but developed it a point further. Revealing the depths of the author's puritanical bent, its theme was universal depravity and the "plot" was very like that of Hawthorne's "Ethan Brand." The speaker, in the pose of the perfect man, supposedly made a research expedition to New York, Washington, Trenton, and elsewhere to examine the conditions of sin in the world, only to find it just as rampant in his own Vermont village and indeed in his own soul. The lecture was delivered in Boston in 1870—appropriately enough, for it satirized the self-righteousness of the New England reformer: "I asked a Boston man, and he indignantly denied that there had been any sin in Boston since Fulton's time."

The reversal in this lecture was a kind of double one. The implication was that the sin of pride is the hardest to get rid of. The lecturer concluded his survey of sin and his lecture in the following words:

I had been horrified at the sin I had seen away; more so at learning that all I had seen abroad was going on regularly at home; and still more so to find that all I had found away and at home existed in full force and vigor in myself; that I cherished and practised in one form or another every sin that I had seen in anybody else. And what humbled me was the fact, that the knowledge that I had all these moral blemishes was not confined to myself. My discovery of the fact was recent—my neighbors had always known it.

I at last found the man of sin. I was the man. I am now busily engaged in reforming,—not the world, but myself,—and I hope I am succeeding. I succeeded in checking myself in time to save lies only yesterday; I am now correcting all errors in accounts that are in my favor; in short, by dint of hard work and careful watching I have got to a point of excellence where it is perfectly safe to say that I am no longer distinctively "the man of sin." My hearers, all of you who try hard enough and watch closely enough, may, in the course of a great many years, if you are gifted and have patience, get to be as good as I am. I know you will shrink from a task so apparently hopeless, but I assure you the reward is great enough to justify the trial.[23]

"In Search of the Man of Sin" was not only a solid and clever satire on human morality, but it was very specific. Cornelius Vanderbilt and the Tammany politicians John Morrisey and Fernando and Benjamin Wood and others were mentioned in a way that today would surely call forth a libel suit. The theme of political and financial corruption was the important issue of the day, and Locke was calling attention to the manipulations outside the control of the Grant administration, especially in state and national legislatures and in the operations of the Tammany Ring.

Though not his most popular lecture, "In Search of the Man of Sin" was Locke's most perfect work—a small masterpiece. It presented a caustic portrait of the moral life of American politics in the Gilded Age. It embodied most of Locke's profoundest moral reflections, concerning both public and private morals. And it showed a subtle mastery of the satiric pose that was unequaled even in the Nasby letters.

CHAPTER 5

Teller of Tales

A S A WRITER OF FICTION, Locke exceeded in quantity what he accomplished in quality. It is impossible to estimate how many short stories, novelettes, and novels he wrote, because many of them were unsigned. In the Plymouth, Bucyrus, and Findlay newspapers, of which he was publisher and editor, it might be assumed that he wrote all the stories that did not bear someone else's name or were not attributed to some other newspaper or magazine. But such an assumption would be reckless. The ethics of newspaper exchange, and journalists' neglect of copyright, made common practice of the reprinting of material without acknowledgment. Also, it was not uncommon for an editor to print the work of an aspiring local writer who might not want his name attached.

On the other hand, it is probable that Locke wrote most of the unsigned material in those papers. In 1858, a rival editor accused him of getting someone else to do his writing, and he replied: "During the last campaign, no one has written for our paper but ourselves, and except four instances, we can say the same for the entire three years we have had charge of it."[1] The "we" in this statement may have included J. G. Robinson, who was then co-publisher of the Bucyrus *Journal;* but Robinson seems to have concerned himself primarily with the printing. The evidence of contemporaries, as well as the fact that Locke reprinted some of the newspaper stories in his books, indicates that at least a good portion of the fiction was his.

The circumstances were different on the Toledo *Blade.* Locke's stories probably had a good deal to do with the phenomenal success of the *Weekly Blade.* But on both the weekly and the daily, he worked with a number of editors and contributors capable of writing salable fiction. And, as those papers increased in physical size and as Locke became more involved in other matters, he wrote a smaller percentage of the total words. It is therefore dangerous to ascribe any particular unsigned story in the *Blade* to him.

Locke's writing was so vast and varied that it is not always possible to classify it strictly by genre. There was, of course, fiction in the Nasby letters. The fables and narrative essays in *The Morals of Abou Ben Adhem* might be considered the author's finest contribution to fiction—aside from the Nasby material. Yet there remains a large body of writing that clearly belongs in the categories of short story, tale, novel, and romance. It falls roughly into three types: the comic story, the melodramatic romance (short or long), and the sociological novel. There is overlapping of the types, however. The sociological novel always has elements of melodrama, and the comic story nearly always criticizes society.

I *Comic Stories*

"Confessions of a Quack," an unsigned story in the Plymouth *Advertiser* may be a youthful example of Locke's comic writing.[2] It told of Doctor Thalaba Killman, who was "to be consulted on every disease to which the human frame is liable, but he had more especially devoted his attention to nervous, chronic, epileptic, intestinal and mental disorders." Dr. Killman's patent nostrum was recommended by numerous testimonials, which he wrote himself:

Manchester, Aug. 4th.

To Dr. Thalaba Killman, Sir: I beg to inform you that some years ago my right ear was most unwarrantably cut off by the sword of a yeomanry soldier. It remained in that state, and I was universally called the cropped donkey, till I was induced to try your esteemed balsam, the effect of which has been such, that my ear has not only grown again but is twice as large as the other.

Your humble servant,
Balaam Freeman.

After years of success and fame, the doctor was accosted and beaten by one of his victims. In a semi-conscious state, he was given some of his own cure. His confessions were written from his bed, from which he knew he would never rise, not because of the beating but because of the medicine. The use of the first person allowed the author to employ the same kind of reverse argument that was later employed in the Nasby letters. Everything that the doctor said was, by implication, to be used against him and his kind. Bitter and merciless as satire, the story was well told—excellent and timely newspaper fiction.

An even more macabre tale was "Tom Long," also in the Plymouth *Advertiser* (April 29, 1854). Like some of Poe's burlesque Gothic tales, it was so fantastically grim as to be comic. The subtitle, "Inconveniences of Dissipation," was a fine stroke of understatement. The hero, in an orgy of drunkenness, was beaten by a saloonkeeper when he attempted to get an after-hours drink on credit. Fearing that he had killed him, the saloonkeeper dragged the "body" to the door of another saloon. The second saloonkeeper discovered him, and from there he was dragged to the cemetery. Finally the hero awoke in the apartment of some medical students who were all ready to begin dissection. His reappearance at the saloons sent the keepers into shock, for they thought he was a ghost. The combination of circumstances reformed Tom, and he never drank again. With this deliberately grotesque plot, and a cast of characters that seemed to come from a drawing by Hogarth, the story moved forward with lively directness. Both the temperance moral and the morbid humor are characteristically David Ross Locke's though this story too is unsigned.

The suggestion of burlesque in "Tom Long" was to be found more positively in "The Bow-Legged Knight," first printed in the Bucyrus *Journal* (October 29, 1858), and later published as one of Nasby's works in *Divers Views, Opinions, and Prophecies.* A later example of the burlesque romance was published "in an Eastern paper" and republished posthumously in the *Weekly Blade* for April 19, 1888. It was headed: "A Fictitious Fact, Being a Tale of Love in Low Life.—Love!—Disappointment!—Treachery!—Death!—Remorse!—More Death!"

Love rules the camp, the court, and various other places, says the poet. I cannot tell the name of the poet, and possibly I have not quoted correctly. I am shaky in quotations. When writing original matter, I never read Shakespeare, Milton, Byron, or Moore, for the reason I might imbibe something of them, and thereby lessen the force and beauty of my own matter.

Bridget Maloney was a maiden over whose head eighteen summers had passed—a great many years ago. She was, though you wouldn't dream of it from her name, a native of the Emerald Isle. The house of Maloney becoming too small for her, she left it, and in due time was domiciled in New York.

The Maloneys, proud as they are, have always recognized the eternal necessities. Bridget was a true Maloney. Food was a necessity. She would rather have dwelt in marble halls, but she was a woman. Women have no votes, consequently, they are not useful to politicians. Being a woman, she could not get on the police force. To accomplish her necessity, she went into a kitchen. Inscrutable are the decrees of fate. Who shall say there is not an over-ruling power?

But she was beautiful. To see her on a Sunday, with the housemaid, arrayed in her mistress's best clothes, was to see a vision of beauty equalled by few and excelled by none. It would have been better, perhaps, had she put on white stockings with her silk dress; but the unities are not always observed. Silk dresses and blue woolen stockings go often together. I have seen such incongruities even in the theatre.

She had money in the savings bank. She was, therefore, beloved.

Dennis Mahoney, policeman on that beat, loved her at first sight. He made inquiries concerning her book at the savings bank, and that love became distraction. He laid siege to her heart. He frequented her kitchen. He ate cold corned beef with her off the kitchen table, and manifested his tenderness in many ways. He took her to balls, where she was observed of all observers. He proposed to her—she accepted him.

But the course of true love never did run smooth. This remark is not mine—I saw it once in a book. But as it is as good as any I can make, I unhesitatingly use it. At a ball she met Patsey McGonigle, and Patsey was entranced. Patsey was a porter in a wholesale pickle warehouse, and was a handsome man. He fell madly in love with her, and—oh! the fickleness

of woman!—she fell madly in love with him. He moved upon her
at once. He proposed. She accepted.

Here is a situation. A girl engaged to two men. It is harrowing,
but it is true.

The next night Dennis called, as was his custom. Bridget was
not cruel. She desired to put him out of his suspense as quickly
as possible. On the same principle, we shoot men through the
head. The head is a vital part.

She told him that she had ceased to love him, and would not
marry him.

"Dost love another?" demanded Dennis.

"I do—devotedly—wildly—madly. Away, man; I would see thee
no more!"

And Dennis left her, grinding his teeth. As he reached the
street the rain was beating furiously and the lightning was
illuminating the air. It was a fit night for the swearing of a
terrible oath, for the formation of a fearful purpose.

Dennis Mahoney stood in the storm, but he heeded it not.
Taking off his coat and vest that he might tear open his shirt
and swear in due form, with one hand in the air, with the other
clenched in his hair, with the pitiless rain beating on his bare
breast and vivid lightning illuminating the scene he swore to
be r-r-revenj'd.

He kept his oath.

The next night Dennis Mahoney was in the familiar kitchen
with Bridget. As nothing had been moved, everything was there.
There was the range, the tin-ware, the table, and the sink. On
that table he had eaten—the sight brought powerful remembrance
to his mind, and he burst into tears. On that table, alas! he
should eat nevermore! nevermore!

"Bridget," said Dennis, "you love me not—let me at least be
your friend. Be my friend."

"It is well," returned the damsel. "While I cannot love you
so long as the visage of the McGonigle is imprinted on this heart,
I can at least respect you; and I will."

"Bridget, your good is ever in my mind; I dream of you by
night and think of you by day, or, as I like to be accurate, dream
by day and think by night, as I have a night beat. Your good
is my study. Bridget, your kindling wood is green, and to start
a fire in the range is difficult. Here is a liquid which I bought
for you—for you—that makes it easy. See, you pour a little on

the wood—you touch a match to it—it burns. Is it not gorgeous?"

As Bridget stooped to examine it, the careful observer, had he been there, would have seen the expression of a demon on his once open countenance.

"I' faith," said Bridget. "But it is mesilf that niver saw the bate uv that."

"Here is a gallon of it—take it—take it—it is affection's last offering."

And he rushed out up the area stairs. As he stood on the top of the area, he looked downward and with his hand clenched in triumph, there came hissing through his teeth the deadly words:

"R-r-reven-ja—ha! ha!"

All night Dennis Mahoney paced his lonely beat. As he passed the house he would pause for a moment to hear the rich voice of McGonigle mingle with the silvery te-he of Bridget.

"Laugh on," he said to himself, "laugh on! Ye will weep anon. R-r-reven-j!"

*   ✲   ✲

It was morning in New York. Dennis Mahoney was about to be relieved, when he heard an angry altercation. He approached cautiously, so as to get near enough to see the fun, and not too near to risk his person. There were blows; and, finally, a pistol shot rang out upon the air, and the party, separating, dispersed. Dennis ran to the spot. There was a man bleeding to death—or, rather the vital spark had fled. Dennis looked at the face. Gracious heavens! it was Patsey McGonigle!

He glared wildly for a moment, and then pulled out his watch. It was a 16 dollar hunter-cased, Swiss watch. He had taken it from a drunken man—but this has nothing to do with the story.

"I have yet time!" he shrieked. "She gets up at six and kindles the fire at seven. It is now a quarter to seven. If this watch is as fast as it always is, I can save her—and marry her."

Away he sped. The gazelle never sped faster. As a speeder he did well. He tore down the street like a madman. Men would have turned and looked at that policeman, had there been any on the street. The house was in sight. One convulsive bound and he was in front of it—another, he was at the top of the area stairs—another, and he had burst the door and was in the kitchen.

"Bridget!" he shrieked.

There was no answer. In the center of the room lay a smouldering mass of kitchen girl and clothes, by the side was a bursted can of kerosene.

"Too late—too late!" he moaned, and looked at his watch. For once it was right. He was too late. Bridget was a cinder.

"Speak to me, Bridget," he moaned, rocking over the charred mass.

But she did not speak to him. Charred masses never do, and it was really absurd of him to ask it.

"Curses on the watch," said he. "I will never gobble a sixteen dollar watch again."

And Dennis Mahoney left that room a crushed man. He went on his beat as usual, but not as before. He didn't pick the pocket of a drunken man that day. He was like one in a dream. He walked about with a vacant look in his face, muttering to himself, "Bridget—three hundred dollars in the savings bank."

And that night there was a row. "This will end it," he said. He did not collar a small boy who was looking on, and rush with him to the station-house, but grasping his club he sailed in. A stone, hurled with terrific force and great precision, struck him in the forehead, and he fell, his club rolling dismally on the pavement. He was taken up. A sweet smile was on his face— his lips were parted, as though he was saying, "Bridget—three hundred dollars in the savings bank."

Having killed off all my characters, I stop. He is a great man who can write of people who are deceased. Patsey was dead, Bridget was dead, and Dennis was dead. But the river runs on, the winds blow, the sun shines, the birds sing, and nature humps herself as usual. What is man, or, rather, what is two men, one woman, and a gallon of kerosene. Life is full of mysteries, and death is a queer go. Let us live as virtuous as circumstances will admit.

Locke's comic writings were always edged with asperity. In "A Fictitious Fact," he not only mocked the popular romance but he maliciously attacked one of his favorite butts, the New York Irish. He almost never wrote for the comic effect alone. It is difficult to find a purely humorous line in any of his work. Mark Twain was wrong when he classed Locke among the humorists of the "mere" sort who never preached.[3] Locke—much more than Clemens—always preached.

Locke was most thoroughly at home in satire. Whether his didacticism was a fault or a virtue depends upon the critic. At any rate, in his satiric approach his preaching was masked by the comic pose. In the first-person testimonial of "Confessions of a Quack," the straightforward narrative of "Tom Long," or the mock-seriousness of "A Fictitious Fact," there was no need for the author to obtrude his morals directly. The implications were obvious, and the reader could take them as he pleased. In his fiction, Locke was most skillful when writing in a comic vein.

II *Romances*

It is somewhat astonishing to see, from a man who could write such sound burlesques of the melodramatic plot and character, that the same man could write romances containing all the coincidences, hairbreadth escapes, maudlin sentiment, and stock characterizations that he ridiculed so well. Yet the great mass of Locke's fiction falls squarely into this category. Locke was concerned with writing what would be read, and seldom with creating lasting literature. It is likely that he wrote more popular fiction of this kind than anything else except editorials. There is hardly an issue of any of the newspapers with which he was connected that does not have at least an installment of a popular romance or a tale in it, and often he was the author. This feature of his journalism—probably more than any other—was what made him so successful with the family newspaper.

Without pretensions to literary art, Locke was not, however, concerned only with giving the public what it wanted. He shared with a great many of his educated contemporaries the attitude that it was their duty to edify the less fortunate. And he also shared the idea that such edification should be in the most pleasant and attractive form. The purpose of *Locke's National Monthly*, for example, was to provide literature "which shall meet the people on their own grounds, which shall be neither above them nor below them, but shall furnish just what they need *now*."[4] Locke's own popular literature always taught a simple moral. And it—unlike his Nasby letters—never contained anything that should not be read by the young girls of the genteel household.

"The Journeyman's Secret" (unsigned, in the Bucyrus *Journal*, July 24, 1856) preached that an uncommunicative exterior may conceal a noble, self-sacrificing soul. It, like most of Locke's romances, was set in an environment familiar to both the author and the reader—in this instance, in a Midwestern printing shop. "The Border Heroine, A Western Story" (unsigned, in the same paper, January 1, 1858) told of the bravery of an Arkansas frontier mother in defending her household from bandits. A similar tale of the sparsely settled rural Midwest was "The Mail Robber" (unsigned, same paper, November 1, 1860), in which a mail carrier foiled a robbery attempt. Any of these tales would make a stock American television show with very little change other than a little more realism in the dialogue.

Despite the settings, the genuine local color was negligible. Similarly, two longer stories by Locke, *John Duncan's Widow* (*Locke's National Monthly*, January to March, 1874) and *Elsey Farm, How It Was Lost and Won* (Toledo *Weekly Blade*, February 16 to March 29, 1888), were set in Midwestern towns but contributed little to the reader's understanding of the region. *Elsey Farm* was set in a small village in northwestern Pennsylvania, and Locke explained his choice of location in the second paragraph of the story:

> Why locate a story in such a village? asks the reader. Why not? The elements of a story are, briefly, Love, Hate, Revenge, Devotion, Sacrifice, Greed. Did you ever see a community so small as not to include within its limits all these elements? Wherever you find twenty persons, you shall find them all, and the most of them wonderfully well developed.
>
> They all existed in Brownhelm, hence, Brownhelm is as good a place in which to locate a story as there is in the world.

The plots of *John Duncan's Widow* and *Elsey Farm* were almost identical. Each involved a beautiful, virtuous heroine whose property was threatened by the wicked financial manipulations of the villain, who sought to force the heroine to marry him by this means. There was a handsome young hero, who was the faithful suitor of the heroine and became her husband in the end, but only through the self-sacrifice of another of her admirers, who remained devoted although he knew his chances with her were nil. The plot was at least as old as the century—it was somewhat reminiscent of Walter Scott—and it was a favorite plot in the stage melodramas of the late nineteenth century. Both stories contained a typical melodramatic climax: The scene in *John Duncan's Widow* was in the courtroom, where the unrequited admirer mysteriously appeared with the evidence that convicted the villain, whereupon the villain murdered him then and there and was taken off to jail. In *Elsey Farm*, the unrequited one appeared suddenly to murder the villain at the church where the fateful marriage ceremony was taking place. Characterization in both stories consisted mostly of references to the "lurid light" in the eye of the villain, a heroine who was "the very flower of all the maidens of the village," and a hero who was "a splendid fellow; a young man of great talent, full of ambition, full of hope, full of good, generous impulses, and full of everything but money."

It is not quite fair to say that Locke's romances were full of everything but esthetic value. They did often deal, however unconvincingly, with contemporary American situations, and they lacked the tacit lasciviousness of the cheaper popular literature. They were and are good examples of the newspaper fiction of the time.

III *Sociological Novels*

Plot and characterization were Locke's primary weaknesses. He was never able to sustain a line of action beyond two or three thousand words without gross improbabilities and obtrusive manipulations. In this characteristic he was similar to the crackerbox humorists with whom he was often classed. Skill with the anecdote and the comic tale seemed to be inimical to the sustained narrative. Nearly all the American humorists—Mark Twain excepted—suffered from the same incapacity.

Serious characterization was equally difficult; for the comic writer could not resist the tendency toward caricature, which destroyed the effect of realism. Locke succeeded in creating only one lasting character, Petroleum V. Nasby. But Nasby was a caricature, a type, a symbol. His traits were simple and constant; they were endlessly displayed in a variety of circumstances, but never developed.

Despite those shortcomings, Locke wrote three novels with a seriousness of purpose that raised them far above his other fiction. They were *A Paper City* (1879), *Strong Heart and Steady Hand* (1888), and *The Demagogue* (1891). The first was the only novel that Locke published in book form during his lifetime. The second ran from May 17, three months after the author's death, to August 2 in the *Weekly Blade* and was never republished. *The Demagogue* was published as a book three years after Locke's death.

In all three novels, local color and a social theme were primary aims, and all else was subordinated to them. In his popular romances, Locke had brought up the problems of alcohol, business frauds, and the limitations of small town life; but his handling of them was not convincing because of improbable circumstances and lack of character motivation. Also, he had used familiar settings, but he did not develop them sufficiently to give the reader a true sense of place, and at best the settings lent a slight verisimilitude to the outrageous plots. The three novels were much more convincing.

The subject of *A Paper City* was Western land speculation. It was the story of the fictitious town of New Canton, "originally the meanest little town in the state of Illinois, which puts New Canton very low in the scale of towns." But the town had delusions of grandeur:

> All the cross-roads of the West expected to become Chicagos, and every man, owning one hundred and sixty acres of land, lived in expectation of seeing, before he should depart, stately buildings upon it, and of selling his ground for more per foot front, than it cost him per acre.

> The following pages simply record the rise, progress and fall of one of the thousands of these "cities," and it has the merit, if no other, of being entirely free from exaggeration.

The main plot and its characters were delineated in the first chapter:

> New Canton was the moon-ribbed, ill-fed ghost of a city—not a one-horse but a one-mule town, begotten by the lying promise of four spectral railroads, on the expectation of an impossible ship-canal. One speculator, with cheek of brass and tongue hung upon swivel; three speculators not so gifted, but equally unscrupulous, with just as little to lose; and one honest but deluded man, adopted the creature, and chattered men into the belief there was stuff in it for a lusty present and a vigorous future.

The glib speculator, Charles Burt, was something of a successful Colonel Sellers but without Sellers' endearing features. But, evil as Burt was, he was not the inhuman monster of Locke's romances. A glimpse of his Connecticut boyhood, a characterization of his hypochondriacal wife, and a revelation of his affair with the young and innocent Emeline Butterfield made him the most believable character in the book. Unfortunately, his repentance at the end, after he had escaped to Europe with part of the loot, was insufficiently motivated and unnecessary to the plot. Colonel Peppernell, one of Burt's unscrupulous cronies, was a gruff and oratorical small-time politician, somewhat reminiscent of Nasby. Mr. Gardiner, the honest but deluded man, was rather less well characterized, though his colorless role was satisfactorily filled.

A secondary plot, loosely but adequately connected with the main plot, contained the love interest. James Gardiner, son of the deluded banker, was very nearly a romantic hero except for his weakness in face of public opinion. Mary Lewis escaped perfection—and bliss—through her inability to withstand her mercenary and domineering mother. The two were married at the very end of the book, but only after considerable compromise. Mary was first married for money to Tom Paddleford, the most thoroughly bad character in the novel, but was finally divorced. James never completely got over his stronger love for Emeline Butterfield, the same girl who innocently exposed Charles Burt.

Thus the novel ended happily, but not unqualifiedly so. The romantic leads were united, but James still dreamed of Emeline.

The bankrupt citizens of New Canton began rebuilding their lives, sadder but wiser men.

As a local-color novel, the book had decided merit. The action could take place at no other time or place than the "West" in the late nineteenth century. The characters were typical; and their behavior, both individually and *en masse,* was drawn by one who knew them profoundly. The dialogue, with some exceptions, was true to the scene; and the occasional use of dialect was effective. The author acknowledged the assistance of "Shirley Dare" (Mrs. Susan C. Dunning Power), who presumably wrote the able descriptions of house furnishings and feminine clothing.[5]

As sociological fiction, *A Paper City* was even stronger. Locke demonstrated his knowledge of small-town manipulators, and the economic conditions that made their existence possible. The social and moral effects of the land boom on the life of a prairie town were made uncompromisingly clear. The chapter depicting the run on Gardiner's bank was the epitome of a typical phenomenon of the 1870's. The novel was strikingly parallel to the series of Nasby letters of 1875, dealing with the paper currency rage. But, whereas the Nasby letters were exaggerated for the sake of satire, the novel attempted to show the sordid realities. *A Paper City* shows Locke in the role of an early Frank Norris, but with a touch of the wit of a Dickens.

Strong Heart and Steady Hand was clearly inferior to *A Paper City;* but, because of its panoramic descriptions of Western travel and its bold social thesis, it should be considered among Locke's serious novels. Its plot was enormously farfetched and its characters never quite came alive, though they exhibited occasional glimmerings of humanness. The reader was never quite told whether or not the heroine had committed carnal sin with the villain. The point was that she deserved a chance to live a normal life in society.

He [the hero, Brooks] could only think of her eyes stained with grief, not sin. He had been with her and her friends for days and had seen no approach to lightness in word or manner, and so slight a girl could hardly be mistress of the art of feigning. The story he heard that afternoon gave him a clew to what had been strange in her conduct. Such a shadow over her, whether deserved or undeserved, was sufficient to make her flee life, and he shuddered to think how close he had been to extremest agony—"deserved." He recalled the word as soon as he thought it. To all his instincts, Miss Winter was a clean, good woman, and he made up his mind (and Brooks could be very stubborn when he took a notion) to be her friend as far as she would let him. With all this weight of ill-report lying against her, it might be she would some day be glad of a faithful friend. And, if in the sad chances of human nature that there was any truth in what was said about her, why, God help her, she needed a friend more than ever, and he would not shrink in her sorest need.

The theme of the novel, then, was the effects of a lost reputation on a woman's life, and the blame was placed, not on the weak woman, but on her seducer and on the society that closed its doors to her.

The action of the story took place from New York to the gold fields of California, and the scenes along the route presented a memorable picture of America on the move in the 1870's. Locke's observations were those of a traveler, not of a local inhabitant. The same eye that made *Nasby in Exile* an excellent travelogue gave immediacy to some of the scenes in *Strong Heart and Steady Hand*. The description of Omaha, on the route of the Union Pacific Railroad, was one of the best:

Omaha, a city of a railroad, and the gateway to a world in the West. A city made up of adventurous men and women—a city that never looks backward, having nothing to look backward to, but whose eye is fixed upon the future. A city with an actual empire in front of it, and an empire that is to be behind it. A city which looks out over thousands of miles of virgin prairie, that has not yet known man, and waits and hopes that they will be possessed and occupied, and in their future it will find its own.

Here, from the outskirts, the great cloth-topped prairie schooners lurched forth for regions north and south of the railroad line. Frontier men in fringed buckskins and slouch hats skulked about on errands for supplies from Arizona or the Texas border, among streets or shops filled with emigrant supplies.

... First he saw the town as everybody does, then he saw the hundred thousand dollar school house on the bluff, then he saw the town from other standpoints, and then he went up to the school house again. The smelting works occupied him one day, and the river, on which there were occasional boats, another. He interviewed Indian hunters and leggined scouts, and looked over the quill work and war clubs in the museum till it grew monotonous, and he had observed the town from all possible points up and down the river.

The story continued with a description of the makeshift emigrant barracks, where five thousand people waited for the railroad line to be repaired some hundreds of miles west. The fact that the observations of Locke's main character were those of a traveler made them all the more American, for most Americans in the West were travelers—enticed by the opportunities, real or imagined, and awed by the vastness, the uncouthness, and the challenge. The novel was certainly an artistic failure because of the absurdities of character and plot—a heartless villain, an old miner seeking revenge, a convenient discovery of gold, and a deadly duel. But at its best the book managed to convey something of a sense of the uprootedness and the restless movement of populations in the period of Western migration.

Locke's most important novel, *The Demagogue*, was subtitled *A Political Novel*. As in his other sociological novels, he was concerned with social problems—of race, women's rights, education, and poverty. And again the regional setting was an integral part of the story; it was set mostly in Locke's own Ohio. But the main object of attack was political patronage and the circumstances that made demagoguery possible in American democracy.

Caleb Mason, the protagonist, was one of Locke's most memorable characters and may well have had his source in some actual Ohio politician. He was born in the Black Swamp in the northern part of the state, and the whole atmosphere of the story was colored by the opening description of the region:

It was eleven o'clock at night, in one of the vast wildernesses that covered North-western Ohio fifty or sixty years ago. It was in November, the most dreary of all the months in that country—

a month when the cold rains fall and are never weary, when Nature is in its most sullen temper, as though sensible that it had made a failure of spring and summer, and it was therefore anxious to wreak its vengeance upon the country by continuing in an ugly mood. The air was cold—so cold that the rain which was falling had changed its mind after leaving the clouds where it was born, and struck the earth in little pellets, just light enough to be carried on the wind, and just heavy enough to cut and bruise like birdshot. The wind, charged with these missiles, was as fierce and as ugly as the rain, and the stinging little particles, too hard for snow and too insignificant for hail, were as disagreeable to unsheltered man and beast as anything could be. They cut like knives, and whoever was exposed to them felt that he was storming a hidden battery, the defenders of which were shooting showers of little lancets from endless rows of mitrailleuses.

The roads were long streaks of mud, half earth and half water, beaten together into a sticky mass, too thick for a boat to float in, and too thin to support the hoofs of a horse. It was a stagger, not a walk or a trot, for the poor beasts condemned to travel these roads. Their advance was a series of lurches, of sinkings and recoveries; and slow indeed was the progress to be made.

On either side of the long line of inky blackness that marked the open way for the traveler, were immense trees—black walnut, oak, ash and hickory—set as closely as possible, compatible with growth and life, their branches interlacing and forming a canopy which held the wet when it was rainy, and kept out the sun when the sky was clear; and all the time sending up clouds of malaria. There was a shake of ague in every drop of the vegetable-impregnated water under foot, and another in every breath of the malaria-laden air above.

The soil was, as a rule, a rich black mould, five to ten feet deep, soft from being so long covered with water; and the land was so level that the falling of a tree centuries ago across a run or creek dammed it, making a swamp of what had once been fair land, and which would be again when the hardy settler, armed with his axe and sustained by quinine, should come and search out the original course of the stream, and by clearing it out, permit the water to flow through its natural channel to seek the river and thence the lake. . . .

The squalid cabin in which Caleb was born "was laziness built of logs; it was unthrift patched, and carelessness with broken windows." The country doctor who was summoned greeted the newborn baby: "Howl away, my fine feller!... howl away! You can't commence howlin' too soon, born as you are in this cheerful country. Howl away! You may have a happy life, but the chances are agin you."

The quick-witted child was thus motivated from the beginning to rise above his surroundings, regardless of how he did it. The scenes in the one-room schoolhouse, where the boy received his early education, further reinforced the authenticity of the setting. And the boy's successful plotting led to the masterful political machinations of the adult. Chapters X through XVII showed Mason's political rise—through marriage into the family that controlled the local machine, through backwoods oratory and attention to appearances, through vote trading and subterfuge—until he became a United States Senator and the power in the political machine. Having espoused Republicanism and the anti-slavery cause from expediency, not principle, his prospects were checked by the assassination of Lincoln—an event that was dramatically depicted in Chapter XVIII. Finally he was exposed by the young lawyer Sam Gleason, the suitor of the woman Mason had jilted in order to marry into money and power. As Mason's constituents, infuriated by knowledge of his crimes, clamored about the doors of the county courthouse, Mason retired to a dark room in the courthouse basement and shot himself.

The ending was overdramatic, and Mason's last-minute return of conscience smacked of poetic justice: "The man of steel found he had a heart at last—something he had been ignorant of.... The most exacting vengeance could have demanded nothing more than he underwent that night before he took the coward's refuge, suicide, from his torture. He had his hell in that one hour before he died." Furthermore, the sympathetic characters in the story all married at the end and presumably lived happily ever after. Yet the character of Caleb Mason, around which the whole story was tightly centered, was

the most fully developed character that Locke ever created. Locke
showed in Mason an awareness of social and psychological forces
acting upon an individual from birth to death. With a few exceptions, Mason's actions were not only credible but probable under
the carefully delineated circumstances. But Mason is more than
an individual. He stands close to Dos Passos' Number One and
to Robert Penn Warren's Willie Stark as representative of an
all too-frequent American phenomenon. He also stands as a
symbol and a warning of perhaps the greatest weakness of
democracy, the flaw perceived by Plato in *The Republic* and by
critics of democratic government ever since—the danger of the
popular leader who becomes a tyrant.

The style of Locke's novels had both the strengths and weaknesses of his haphazard education. At its best, it had the colorful
directness of common American speech. In *The Demagogue*,
for example, he characterized a Democratic community in Ohio,
which Caleb Mason meant to convert: "There had never been
as yet but one Whig candidate who had the audacity to
attempt a speech in that neigborhood, and as the free citizens,
headed by Bill Sampsell, had tarred and feathered him, the
candidates who came after did not feel very much like attempting
the political missionary business in that locality." And in *A
Paper City* he described the houses of the prairie town: "Beside
the honest, weatherbeaten walls, the patchy red and white of
such as had been painted and peeled looked as though they
had an attack of timber-measels, and never got over it." But
there were also numerous awkwardnesses that reflected haste
and a somewhat shaky command of syntax and verb forms.

Unlike some of his contemporaries, Locke did not experiment
with point of view in his novels. In his comic stories he had
used a straight first-person narrator or had assumed the mock-
attitude of burlesque. But in the romances and the sociological
novels, the author was omniscient. The story was strictly in the
third person, the author frequently inserted his own thoughts,
and there was little attempt to get inside the consciousness of
the characters. In view of Locke's remarkable success with the
Nasby letters and with the reverse logic of his lectures, it is too

bad that he did not attempt a more sophisticated approach to point of view in the novel. This failure goes far in explaining his failure to achieve the first rank in American fiction.

He was almost equally out of touch with emerging attitudes toward literary symbolism. He used the stock symbols of nine-teenth-century fiction—most notably the weather. Both weather and region in the opening lines of *The Demagogue* illustrate his use of symbols at its best, and are susceptible of lengthy interpretation. *Strong Heart and Steady Hand* contained Locke's most vigorous efforts in the direction of modern symbolism. In that story was a scene involving Marian Winter and Henry Brooks on a California mountain, where the two were reminded of the Mount of Transfiguration, and where they appeared to be cleansed and purified before their descent. It is tempting to identify Marian with Mary Magdalen and Henry with Christ. Indeed, Henry remained strangely benign and aloof when Marian married their mutual friend, Jarvas Lord, in the end. But almost certainly, Locke had not worked out any complete signification in his own mind.

As in so much of his other work, Locke missed the first rank of literary excellence through a want of finish and sophistication. His most earnest efforts in fiction deserve a better fate than they have yet received, but they are nevertheless hastily done with more sensitiveness to the popular reading public than to artistic merit. But as representative of the struggles of a serious and enlightened mind with the problems of the late-nineteenth-century novel, and as documents in the history of American politics and society, they deserve recognition.

IV Achievement

Of course, Locke's greatest achievement was not in the writing of fiction. His reputation ought properly to rest on his record as a whole—as an American, as a journalist, as the creator of Nasby.

As a representative American, he had risen from the ranks to both riches and fame. A Horatio Alger hero, he had applied the materialistic advice of Benjamin Franklin and had won his way by hard, honest toil. But he was much more than an Alger hero. Indeed, he could see the less glittering side of the Alger myth, and the protagonist of his *The Demagogue* has been called "an Alger boy gone sour."[6] If he did not attain the many-sided greatness of the eighteenth-century Franklin, he came close to it. He could not slough off the American Puritan guilt complex as could Franklin, nor could he command the cool rationality—he was always a violent partisan. But his accomplishments in literature, journalism, business, and social betterment were unequaled by anyone in his own age who attempted as much. Always practical, always active, he nevertheless set forth from firm and rational principles. Even in his shortcomings—his excessive materialism, his alcoholism, and a certain esthetic insensitiveness—he typified American ideals better than the well-bred and well-schooled New Englander, the Southern patrician, or the numerous Western wits.

Locke was a great newspaperman. Under his leadership, the Toledo *Blade* became well known throughout the Central and Midwestern states and was read from coast to coast. It contributed vitally to both the forming and carrying out of public opinion in the 1870's and 1880's. Without Locke, the Republican Party would have lacked one of its most effective members. Without Locke, the American people would have lacked one of their most effective educative influences.

Locke was a great political satirist. Although he swung untold influence in his editorials and other writings, the Nasby letters were his best weapon. He worked the old saw about the power of the pen to its fullest. He made "humor" a threat to be reckoned with. The ridicule of the Nasby letters must have turned many a lukewarm patriot into a militant anti-reactionary, and must have played a significant part in gaining and consolidating the results of the Civil War and the reforms that eventually followed.

Both as the writer of the Nasby letters and as lecturer "Nasby," Locke fastened upon a well-deserved, if precarious, place in American literature. Though the letters were primarily propaganda, the author—almost in spite of himself—employed unique literary craft that made Petroleum V. Nasby an American symbol.

What was voluminously conveyed in the letters was condensed to essence in Locke's lectures. The popular lecture was an ephemeral medium. Few if any of the utterances of the once famous kings of the platform are read today. Even the masterpieces of Artemus Ward and Mark Twain are watery without the voice and manner of their originators to give them life. But not so with the lectures of "Nasby." Though "Cussid Be Canaan" and "In Search of the Man of Sin" are known today only by a few dusty scholars, they retain most, if not all, of their original impact. Even when silently read, they are an authoritative voice from the past—the past which has shaped the present. And besides, they have a living message for today.

Locke's fiction and poetry may not deserve the close scrutiny of busy modern men. They may remain in the shady realm of the second rank, to be observed as products of a roiling and teeming period of the American adventure. But Locke the man, Locke the lecturer, and the inveterate Petroleum V. Nasby may justly claim their places even in an age of masses and machines, atomic bombs and automation.

Notes and References

Chapter One

1. "Always Begin Right," Plymouth, Ohio, *Advertiser*, October 22, 1853, p. 1.
2. MS letter from Nathaniel Locke to David Ross Locke, no date, in the Rutherford B. Hayes Library, Fremont, Ohio.
3. *"Grip's" Historical Souvenir of Marathon* (1900), pp. 19-20, 70.
4. *Ibid.*, p. 82.
5. For my description of the Cortland *Democrat*, I am indebted to John M. Harrison and William W. Austin, and to Mrs. Dorothea B. Jackson of the Cortland County Historical Society.
6. MS letter from D. R. Locke to James and Ruth Locke, January 26, 1851, in the Rutherford B. Hayes Library.
7. John M. Killits, *Toledo and Lucas County, Ohio, 1623-1923* (Chicago, 1923), p. 491.
8. "Valedictory," Plymouth *Advertiser*, December 6, 1855, p. 2.
9. "Nebraska and Slavery," Plymouth *Advertiser*, January 14, 1854, p. 2.
10. "Annexation in General," Plymouth *Advertiser*, January 21, 1854, p. 2. "Women's Rights," April 8, 1854, p. 2. "To Whiskey Drinkers," May 13, 1854, p. 2.
11. Plymouth *Advertiser*, November 19, 1853, p. 2, and May 6, 1854, p. 2.
12. MS letter, November 13, 1864, in the Rutherford B. Hayes Library.
13. Cited in "Papers and Memorabilia of David Ross Locke (Petroleum V. Nasby), 1833-1888, Robinson Locke (Rodney Lee), 1856-1920," in the Rutherford B. Hayes Library.
14. Quoted in George W. Cable, *Mark Twain and George W. Cable* (East Lansing, Michigan, 1960), p. 74.
15. The articles appeared in the Mansfield, Ohio, *Herald* for October 3, October 31, and probably November 7, 1855. Part of the second and all of the presumed third article are missing from the files in the Mansfield Public Library. At least one Sniggs letter (discovered by John Harrison) had been published earlier—in the Plymouth *Advertiser*, November 3, 1854, p. 2.
16. "To the Patrons of the Herald," Mansfield *Herald*, September

12, 1855, p. 2. Roeliff Brinkerhoff, *Recollections of a Lifetime* (Cincinnati, 1900), pp. 94-98.

17. "Wanted Immediately," Bucyrus, Ohio, *Journal*, January 1, 1858, p. 2.

18. Robert S. Harper, *The Ohio Press in the Civil War* (Columbus, Ohio, 1962), p. 8.

19. Bucyrus *Journal*, December 21, 1861, p. 2.

20. Cyril Clemens, *Petroleum V. Nasby* (Webster Groves, Missouri, 1936), p. 21. The governor mentioned is "Bough" (Brough), who was not governor until 1864. Clemens' source is probably Emily S. Bouton, "David Ross Locke," Toledo *Blade*, February 15, 1888, p. 4, though the story was frequently reprinted. The signed commission of 1861 is in the Rutherford B. Hayes Library.

21. He wrote a tribute to Willie Locke Robinson, son of J. G. Robinson, who drowned November 23 at the age of four. (Bucyrus *Journal*, November 29, 1861, p. 3.)

22. Reprinted in Allen Thorndike Rice (ed.), *Reminiscences of Abraham Lincoln by Distinguished Men of His Time* (New York, 1886), pp. 439-53.

23. The date given by Harrison is October 15, but that was a Sunday, when no paper was issued. There is no notice in the paper itself of Locke's editorship.

On Locke's residence in Findlay, see William D. Humphrey, *Findlay, the Story of a Community* (Findlay, Ohio, 1961). There is almost no information on the Bellefontaine period of Locke's life, and the files of the *Republican* are not extant for 1865. See W. F. Gilkison, "Recollections of Nasby," Indianapolis *News*, March 13, 1888.

On the reprinting of the Nasby letters in other newspapers, see Locke's letter to the New York *Tribune*, October 9, 1864 (MS in the Columbia University Library), in which he asks that the New York paper print the Nasby letters regularly.

24. William H. Taft, "David Ross Locke: Forgotten Editor," *Journalism Quarterly*, XXXIV (Spring, 1957), 205.

25. "Business Notice," Toledo *Blade*, August 16, 1865, p. 2.

26. Cable, pp. 73-74.

27. *Toledo Weekly Blade (Nasby's Paper), Its Rise and Progress* (Toledo, 1885), in the Rutherford B. Hayes Library.

28. Cited in Milton Meltzer, *Mark Twain Himself* (New York, 1960), p. 116.

29. Cable, pp. 73-75.

30. James Burton Pond, *Eccentricities of Genius* (New York, 1900),

p. 193. Paul Fatout, *Mark Twain on the Lecture Circuit* (Bloomington, Indiana, 1960), pp. 149-50. Samuel L. Clemens, *Mark Twain's Autobiography* (New York, 1924), pp. 156-57.

31. Meltzer, p. 116.

32. "Notes and Comments," *Locke's National Monthly*, III (June, 1875), 287.

33. Cyril Clemens, p. 117. For a few cryptic notes on Locke's life in the city, see MS letters from Locke to "Miss Joy," December 9, 1870, and to John M. Morris, February 14, 1871, in the Rosenburg Library, Galveston, Texas; from Locke to unknown correspondent, 1872 (no day given), and to Horatio C. King, February 16, 1876, in the Yale University Library; and from Locke to Whitelaw Reid, February 8, 1874, and April 24, 1874, in The Pierpont Morgan Library.

34. See MS letters from Thomas Nast to D. R. Locke, March 23 and May 20, 1867, in the Rutherford B. Hayes Library. See also "Nast," Toledo *Blade*, November 2, 1872, p. 4.

35. Quoted in Cable, p. 73. On the medical college and the gas company, see Clark Waggoner (ed.), *History of Toledo and Lucas County, Ohio* (New York, 1888), p. 555. On Locke's finances, see MSS in the Rutherford B. Hayes Library. On the typewriter, see the Toledo *Blade*, June 21, 1947. On the sewing machine, see Joseph Jones (ed.), *The Struggles of Petroleum V. Nasby* (Boston, 1963), p. 245, and recurrent ads in the *Weekly Blade*, 1887.

36. "Prospectus," *The Index*, I (January 1, 1870), 5. See also Frank Luther Mott, *A History of American Magazines* (Cambridge, Massachusetts, 1938), III, 78.

37. "Neil Burgess, and His New Play," New York *Mirror*, August 9, 1879, p. 6.

38. G. C. D. Odell, *Annals of the New York Stage* (New York, 1927-49), XI, 41, passim. John Bouvé Clapp and Edwin F. Edgett, *Players of the Present* (New York, 1899), pp. 30, 47.

39. Toledo *Blade*, February 15, 1888, p. 4.

Chapter Two

1. *Nasby in Exile* (Toledo, 1882), p. 460.

2. Marvin Meyers, *The Jacksonian Persuasion* (New York, 1960), p. 10.

3. Bucyrus, Ohio, *Journal*, July 24, 1856, p. 1.

4. "The Courier and the Nigger," Findlay, Ohio, *Hancock Jeffersonian*, February 14, 1862, p. 2.

5. "Unreal Victory," Bucyrus *Journal,* November 12, 1858, p. 2.

6. "Secession in a New Spot," Bucyrus *Journal,* December 13, 1860. Reprinted in Harvey S. Ford (ed.), *Civil War Letters of Petroleum V. Nasby* (Columbus, Ohio, 1962).

7. "The Fremont Affair," October 25, 1861, p. 2; "Wanted—A General," November 1, 1861, p. 2; "The Removal of Fremont," November 8, 1861, p. 2, Bucyrus *Journal.* "An Advance Wanted," January 3, 1862, p. 2; "The Dance of Death," February 14, 1862, p. 2, *Hancock Jeffersonian.*

8. "The Campaign," *Hancock Jeffersonian,* September 16, 1864, p. 2.

9. "Phillips Furious," Toledo *Blade,* January 15, 1866, cited in John M. Harrison, "David Ross Locke and the Fight on Reconstruction," *Journalism Quarterly,* XXXIX (Autumn, 1962), 492-93.

10. *Swingin' Round the Cirkle* (Boston, 1867), pp. 210-11.

11. "Cussid Be Canaan," *The Struggles of Petroleum V. Nasby* (Boston, 1888), pp. 658-59.

12. John McElroy, *Andersonville* (Toledo, 1879), p. xvi. Toledo *Blade,* July 6, 1880, p. 2.

13. *Divers Views, Opinions, and Prophecies of Petroleum V. Nasby* (Cincinnati, 1866), pp. 46-47.

14. "Corruption in Congress," Toledo *Blade,* March 1, 1870, p. 2.

15. *The President's Policy* (Toledo, 1877), p. 3.

16. "Financial Legislation," Toledo *Blade,* July 2, 1872, p. 2.

17. "In Action Two Minutes," Toledo *Blade,* June 29, 1872, p. 3. "The Railroad Problem," Toledo *Blade,* December 28, 1880, p. 2.

18. *The Nasby Letters* (Toledo, 1893), p. 509, from the Toledo *Blade,* December 19, 1887.

19. *The Nasby Letters,* p. 125.

20. "Female Suffrage in Toledo," Toledo *Blade,* November 5, 1872, p. 2; "Woman Suffrage," Toledo *Blade,* November 8, 1872, p. 2.

21. *The Nasby Letters,* p. 142.

22. "Catholicism and Ignorance," Plymouth, Ohio, *Advertiser,* December 3, 1853, p. 2. But see "A Merry Christmas to All" and "Religious Persecution" in the Toledo *Blade,* December 24, 1880, p. 4.

23. *Nasby in Exile,* p. 372. See Emily S. Bouton, "David Ross Locke," Toledo *Blade,* February 15, 1888, p. 4, for the story of Locke's escape from England. See James B. Pond, *Eccentricities of Genius* (New York, 1900), on Redpath's influence.

24. *The Nasby Letters,* pp. 459-60.

25. "Rum in Politics," Toledo *Blade*, November 8, 1884. See "Liquor and Politics," *Weekly Blade*, September 27, 1883.

Chapter Three

1. Seba Smith, Preface to *My Thirty Years out of the Senate*, cited in Walter Blair, *Native American Humor* (New York, 1937), p. 40.

2. "Introduction," *The Biglow Papers, Second Series,* in *The Poetical Works of James Russell Lowell* (Boston, 1890), p. 232.

3. Charles Farrar Browne, *Artemus Ward: His Book* (New York, 1862), pp. 176, 186.

4. Cyril Clemens, *Petroleum V. Nasby* (Webster Groves, Missouri, 1936), pp. 114-16. Jack Clifford Ransome, "The Career of David Ross Locke and Its Significance" (unpublished M. A. thesis, University of Toledo, 1947), p. 17.

5. Quoted in Emily S. Bouton, "David Ross Locke," Toledo *Blade*, February 15, 1888, p. 4. See Harvey S. Ford (ed.), *Civil War Letters of Petroleum V. Nasby* (Columbus, Ohio, 1962), pp. 5-7.

6. *The Struggles of Petroleum V. Nasby* (Toledo, 1880), pp. 261-62.

7. *The Nasby Letters* (Toledo, 1893), p. 195.

8. *Ibid.,* p. 161.

9. *The Struggles,* pp. 56-57.

10. *Divers Views, Opinions, and Prophecies of Petroleum V. Nasby* (Cincinnati, 1866), pp. 68-70, 416-19. *The Nasby Letters,* pp. 229-31, 371-73.

11. *The Struggles,* pp. 81-82.

12. *Ibid.,* pp. 143-45.

13. *Ibid.,* pp. 292-95.

14. *Ibid.,* pp. 120-21.

15. *The Nasby Letters,* p. 202.

16. John M. Harrison, "David Ross Locke and the Fight on Reconstruction" (unpublished M. A. thesis, State University of Iowa, 1961), p. 41.

17. MS beginning "The Institoot is progressing ... " in the Rutherford B. Hayes Library. The letter was printed in *Struggles,* pp. 395-99. See also MS of "To Gen Ulissis S Grant" in the Yale University Library.

18. *The Nasby Letters*, p. 431.
19. *Ibid.*, p. 392.
20. *The Struggles*, p. 7.
21. *Swingin' Round the Cirkle* (Boston, 1867), p. 79.
22. *The Nasby Letters*, p. 271.
23. *Ibid.*, p. 484.
24. "Rev. Robert McCune's," Toledo *Blade*, February 18, 1888, p. 6.
25. Toledo Blade Co., *Toledo Weekly Blade (Nasby's Paper), Its Rise and Progress* (Toledo, 1885), p. 6.
26. *The Struggles*, pp. 67-68. See Charles H. Wesley, *Ohio Negroes in the Civil War* (Columbus, Ohio, 1962), p. 6.
27. *The Struggles*, pp. 50-51.
28. *Ibid.*, p. 441.
29. *Ibid.*, pp. 188-89.
30. *Ibid.*, p. 265.
31. *The Nasby Letters*, p. 339.
32. *The Struggles*, p. 360.

Chapter Four

1. *Nasby in Exile* (Toledo, 1882), pp. v-vi.
2. *Ibid.*, pp. 372-73.
3. *Ibid.*, p. 510.
4. *Ibid.*, pp. 264-65.
5. *The Morals of Abou Ben Adhem* (Boston, 1875), pp. 230-31.
6. *Ibid.*, p. 132.
7. *Ibid.*, pp. 75-76.
8. *Ibid.*, p. 34.
9. *Ibid.*, p. 150.
10. Cited in Theodore Clarke Smith, *The Life and Letters of James Abram Garfield* (New York, 1925), II, 751.
11. Cited in "Neil Burgess, and His New Play," New York *Mirror*, August 9, 1879, p. 6. The preceding quotation and most of the details of this and the next paragraph are from the same article.
12. George Clinton Odell, *Annals of the New York Stage* (New York, 1927-49), XI, 42.
13. "The Week at the Theatres," New York *Mirror*, March 20, 1880, p. 7. "General Mention," New York *Times*, April 13, 1886, p. 4.
14. *Mark Twain's Autobiography* (New York, 1924), pp. 148-49. See pp. 156-57.
15. *The Struggles of Petroleum V. Nasby* (Boston, 1888), p. 629.

16. *Ibid.*, p. 630.
17. *Ibid.*, pp. 654-55.
18. *Ibid.*, pp. 655-56.
19. *Ibid.*, p. 659.
20. *Ibid.*, p. 661.
21. *Ibid.*, p. 662. Compare Twain's "Speech at the Scottish Banquet in London" (1875), but substantially the same toast was printed in the Toledo *Weekly Blade,* January 7, 1874.
22. *The Struggles* (1888), p. 684.
23. *Ibid.*, p. 715.

Chapter Five

1. "Editorial Courtesy," Bucyrus, Ohio, *Journal,* November 5, 1858, p. 2.
2. Plymouth, Ohio, *Advertiser,* November 5, 1853, p. 1. See also "Our First Page," p. 3: "The tale 'Confessions of a Quack,' we consider most excellent, and though first published some years [*sic*] is a capital hit at the present day of nostrums and quack medicines."
3. Samuel L. Clemens, *Mark Twain in Eruption* (New York, 1940), p. 202.
4. "Notes and Comments," *Locke's National Monthly,* III (May, 1875), 240.
5. Joseph Jones, "Petroleum V. Nasby Tries the Novel," *Texas Studies in English,* XXX (1951), p. 206.
6. *Ibid.*, p. 205.

Selected Bibliography

The most important sources for both Locke's works and information about him are the files of the following newspapers:

Cortland, New York, *Democrat*, 1845-50
Corning, New York, *Fountain of Temperance*, 1850
Pittsburgh *Chronicle*, 1851-53
Plymouth, Ohio, *Advertiser*, 1853-55
Mansfield, Ohio, *Herald*, 1855-56
Bucyrus, Ohio, *Journal*, 1856-61
Findlay, Ohio, *Hancock Jeffersonian*, 1861-65
Toledo, Ohio, *Blade*, 1865-88
Toledo *Weekly Blade*, 1865-88
New York *Evening Mail*, 1871-79

To this should be added *Locke's National Monthly*, 1872-76. No attempt has ever been made to collect Locke's contributions to other newspapers, magazines, and almanacs. Virtually all the Nasby letters first appeared in the *Hancock Jeffersonian* and the *Weekly Blade*.

The only sizable collection of Locke manuscripts is in the Rutherford B. Hayes Library in Fremont, Ohio. The Locke family possess a few papers, and scattered manuscript letters are listed in Joseph Jones, ed., *American Literary Manuscripts* (Austin, Texas, 1960).

Bibliographies are to be found in Daniel Ryan, *The Civil War Literature of Ohio* (Cleveland, 1911); Cyril Clemens, *Petroleum Vesuvius Nasby* (Webster Groves, Missouri, 1936); Walter Blair, *Native American Humor* (New York, 1937); Jack Clifford Ransome, "The Career of David Ross Locke and Its Significance" (unpublished M. A. thesis, University of Toledo, 1947); and John M. Harrison, "David Ross Locke and the Fight on Reconstruction" (unpublished M. A. thesis, State University of Iowa, 1961).

The following list is made up of the earliest identified edition of each of Locke's works. Locke published most of his volumes in several editions with different publishers and often in condensed or expanded forms.

PRIMARY SOURCES

The Nasby Papers. Indianapolis: C. O. Perrine & Co., 1864.

Divers Views, Opinions, and Prophecies of Yours Trooly, Petroleum V. Nasby. Cincinnati: Carroll & Co., 1866.

Androo Johnson, His Life. New York: J. C. Haney & Co., 1866.

Swingin' Round the Cirkle. Boston: Lee and Shepard, 1867.

Ekkoes from Kentucky. Boston: Lee and Shepard, 1868.

The Impendin Crisis uv the Democracy. Toledo: Miller, Locke & Co., 1868.

The Struggles (Social, Financial and Political) of Petroleum V. Nasby. Boston: I. N. Richardson and Company, 1872.

The Morals of Abou Ben Adhem. Boston: Lee and Shepard, Publishers, 1875.

Inflation at the Cross Roads. New York: American News Company, 1875.

The President's Policy. Toledo: Blade Company, 1877.

A Paper City. New York: Dillingham, 1879.

The Democratic John Bunyan. Toledo: Toledo Blade Company, 1880.

The Diary of an Office Seeker. Toledo: Blade Company, 1881.

Hannah Jane. Boston: Lee and Shepard, Publishers, 1882.

Nasby in Exile; or, Six Months of Travel. Toledo: Locke Publishing Company, 1882.

Essay on Lincoln in *Reminiscences of Abraham Lincoln by Distinguished Men of His Time*, ed. ALLEN THORNDIKE RICE. New York: North American Publishing Company, 1886, pp. 439-53.

"Prohibition," *North American Review*, CXLIII (October, 1886), 382-97.

The Struggles (Social, Financial and Political) of Petroleum V. Nasby. Boston: Lee and Shepard, Publishers, 1888. Contains the same material as the 1872 edition plus the three lectures.

The Demagogue. Boston: Lee and Shepard, Publishers, 1891.

The Nasby Letters. Toledo: The Toledo Blade Co., 1893.

Let's Laugh. Girard, Kansas: Appeal to Reason, 1924. Cheap paper reprint of part of *Divers Views*.

Civil War Letters of Petroleum V. Nasby, ed. HARVEY S. FORD. Columbus: Ohio State University Press, 1962. A small collection of letters from *The Struggles* plus "Secession in a New Spot" and an introduction by the editor.

The Struggles of Petroleum V. Nasby, ed. JOSEPH JONES with notes by GUNTHER BARTH. Boston: Beacon Press, 1963. An abridged edition with a good introduction by Jones.

SECONDARY SOURCES

ANON. Article on Locke's ownership of first typewriter in Toledo, Toledo *Blade,* June 21, 1947.

ANON. "Mr. Nasby's Humors," *Nation,* III (December 20, 1866), 491-92. Essay review of Sixth Edition of *Divers Views.*

ANON. *Toledo Weekly Blade (Nasby's Paper), Its Rise and Progress.* Toledo: Toledo Blade Co., 1885. A promotional pamphlet, an important source of material on D. R. Locke, Robinson Locke, and the *Weekly Blade,* but not altogether reliable.

BLAIR, WALTER. *Native American Humor (1800-1900).* New York: American Book Company, 1937. Scholarly estimate of Locke and his relation to the tradition of American humor.

————. "The Popularity of Nineteenth Century American Humorists," *American Literature,* III (May, 1931), 175-94. Study of American humor on the stage, in newspapers and magazines, in books, and on the lecture circuit.

BRINKERHOFF, ROELIFF. *Recollections of a Lifetime.* Cincinnati: Robert Clarke Company, 1900. Reminiscences by one of Locke's partners on the Mansfield, Ohio, *Herald.*

CABLE, GEORGE WASHINGTON. *Mark Twain and G. W. Cable.* East Lansing: Michigan State University Press, 1960. Contains a revealing letter on Cable's visit to Nasby in 1884.

CARPENTER, FRANCIS BICKNELL. *Six Months in the White House.* New York: Hurd and Houghton, 1866. A firsthand account of Lincoln's admiration of "Nasby."

CLAPP, JOHN BOUVÉ, and EDWIN F. EDGETT, *Players of the Present.* New York: The Dunlap Society, 1899. Contains material on Neil Burgess and the performance of Locke's *Widow Bedott.*

CLEMENS, CYRIL. *Petroleum Vesuvius Nasby.* Webster Groves, Missouri: International Mark Twain Society, 1936. A spirited biography of Locke, but it relies partly on untrustworthy sources.

CLEMENS, SAMUEL L. *The Love Letters of Mark Twain.* New York: Harper & Brothers, 1949. Some details of Clemens' acquaintance with Locke.

————. *Mark Twain in Eruption.* New York: Grosset & Dunlap, Publishers, 1940. Clemens' views on American humorists, including Locke.

————. *Mark Twain's Autobiography.* New York: Harper & Brothers, 1924. Fine descriptions of "Nasby" the lecturer.

————. *Mark Twain's Letters.* New York: Harper & Brothers, 1917. Some details of Clemens' acquaintance with Locke.

CLEMENS, WILL M. *Famous Funny Fellows.* Cleveland: William W. Williams, 1882. Notes and anecdotes on American humorists.

"David Ross Locke," *Historical Hand-Atlas.* Chicago: H. H. Hardesty & Co., Publishers, 1882. Some biographical details about Locke.

ESTES, JOSEPH A. "David Ross Locke," *Dictionary of American Biography.* A competent short biography but repeats some earlier myths.

FATOUT, PAUL. *Mark Twain on the Lecture Circuit.* Bloomington: Indiana University Press, 1960. Contains some otherwise unknown details of Locke's life.

FORD, ROBERT. *American Humourists, Recent and Living.* Paisley, Scotland: Alexander Gardner, 1897. Commentary on Locke; nothing new.

HARPER, ROBERT S. *Lincoln and the Press.* New York: McGraw-Hill Book Company, Inc., 1951. Dispels Ida M. Tarbell's conjectures about Locke's relations with Lincoln.

HARRISON, JOHN M. "David Ross Locke and the Fight on Reconstruction," *Journalism Quarterly*, XXXIX (Autumn, 1962), 491-99. Thoroughly reliable study of Locke's change in attitude toward Andrew Johnson—based on the dissertation below.

————. "David Ross Locke and the Fight on Reconstruction." Unpublished M. A. thesis, State University of Iowa, 1961. The soundest scholarly study of Locke to date.

HAYES, RUTHERFORD B. *Diary and Letters of Rutherford B. Hayes.* Columbus: The Ohio State Archaeological and Historical Society, 1925. Mention of a visit of Locke to Hayes in 1885.

HOOPER, OSMAN C. *History of Ohio Journalism, 1793-1933.* Columbus: The Ohio State University Press, 1933. Account of Locke's contribution to Ohio newspapers.

HOWELLS, WILLIAM DEAN. *Stories of Ohio.* New York: American Book Company, 1897. Very inaccurate account of Locke as an important Ohioan.

HUDSON, FREDERIC. *Journalism in the United States.* New York:

Harper & Brothers, 1873. An interview with "Nasby" and biographical material.

HUMPHREY, WILLIAM D. *Findlay, the Story of a Community*. Findlay, Ohio: The Findlay Printing & Supply Co., 1961. Details concerning Locke's residence in Findlay.

JONES, JOSEPH. "Petroleum V. Nasby Tries the Novel: David Ross Locke's Excursions into Political and Social Fiction," *Texas Studies in English*, XXX (1951), 202-18. Excellent assessment of *A Paper City* and of *The Demagogue*.

KILLITS, JOHN M. *Toledo and Lucas County, Ohio, 1623-1923*. Chicago: S. J. Clarke Publishing Co., 1923. Considerable biographical information about Locke.

LANDON, MELVILLE D. *Kings of the Platform and Pulpit*. Chicago: F. C. Smedley and Company, 1891. Information on Locke as lecturer.

LIBRARY OF CONGRESS. "Acquisition Notes," *Information Bulletin*, XVII, Number 49 (December 8, 1958). Description of Lincoln's copy of *The Nasby Papers*.

"Locke, David Ross," *The Biographical Encyclopaedia of Ohio of the Nineteenth Century*. Cincinnati: Galaxy Publishing Company, 1876. Some biographical details about Locke.

LOWELL, JAMES RUSSELL. "Introduction," *The Biglow Papers, Second Series*, in *The Poetical Works of James Russell Lowell*. Boston: Houghton, Mifflin and Company, 1890. Lowell's salute to "Nasby" as political satirist.

MARCHMAN, WATT P. "David Ross Locke," *Museum Echoes*, XXX, Number 5 (May, 1957), 35-38. Brief assessment of Locke's accomplishments.

McELROY, JOHN. *Andersonville; A Story of Rebel Military Prisons*. Toledo: D. R. Locke, 1879. Contains an "Introduction" by Robert McCune and an "Author's Preface" which tell of Locke's part in the publication of the book.

MELTZER, MILTON. *Mark Twain Himself*. New York: Thomas Y. Crowell Company, 1960. Contains description of Locke.

MOTT, FRANK LUTHER. *American Journalism*. New York: Macmillan, 1950. Mention of the New York *Evening Mail*, the Toledo *Weekly Blade*, and D. R. Locke.

————. *A History of American Magazines*. Cambridge: Harvard University Press, 1938–. Material on Locke's connections with *Yankee Notions*, *The Index*, and the Toledo *Blade*.

Selected Bibliography

National Cyclopaedia of American Biography. New York: James T. White, 1896. Articles on Neil Burgess and G. W. N. Yost throw light on Locke's relations with these men.

ODELL, GEORGE CLINTON DENSMORE. *Annals of the New York Stage.* New York: Columbia University Press, 1927-49. Records of the New York performances of *Widow Bedott.*

PAINE, ALBERT BIGELOW. *Thomas Nast—His Period and His Pictures.* New York: The Macmillan Co., 1904. A few details on Nast's acquaintance with Locke.

POND, JAMES BURTON. *Eccentricities of Genius.* New York: G. W. Dillingham Company, 1900. Details on Locke's life, especially as a lecturer.

Portrait and Biographical Record of City of Toledo and Lucas and Wood Counties. Chicago: Chapman Publishing Company, 1895. A few details of Locke's life.

RANSOME, JACK CLIFFORD. "The Career of David Ross Locke and Its Significance." Unpublished M. A. thesis, University of Toledo, 1947. A good compilation of previously published material on Locke.

—————. "David Ross Locke, Civil War Propagandist," *Northwest Ohio Quarterly,* XX, Number 1 (January, 1948), 5-19. Study of Locke's politics during the Civil War, based on the thesis above.

—————. "David Ross Locke, The Post-War Years," *Northwest Ohio Quarterly,* XX, Number 3 (Summer, 1948), 144-58. Study of Locke's life and politics after the Civil War, based on the thesis above.

ROURKE, CONSTANCE. *American Humor.* New York: Harcourt, Brace and Company, 1931. The classic study of American humor, with but brief comments on Nasby particularly.

SCRIBNER, HARVEY, ed. *Memoirs of Lucas County and the City of Toledo.* Madison, Wisconsin: Western Historical Association, 1910. Biographical details on Locke, not necessarily reliable.

TAFT, WILLIAM H. "David Ross Locke: Forgotten Editor," *Journalism Quarterly,* XXXIV (Spring, 1957), 202-7. Sound study of Locke as editor of the Toledo *Blade,* based on the thesis below.

—————. "The *Toledo Blade*: Its First One Hundred Years, 1835-1935." Unpublished Ph. D. dissertation, Western Reserve University, 1950. Includes survey of Locke's editorship of the *Blade.*

TANDY, JENNETTE. *Crackerbox Philosophers in American Humor and Satire.* New York: Columbia University Press, 1925. Still one of the best studies of the tradition of American humor.

Toledo *Blade,* February 15-20, 1888. Contains several articles, memoirs, and tributes to Locke, not available elsewhere.

Toledo *Weekly Blade,* February 23, 1888. Contains several of the same items on Locke that appeared in the daily, with some additions.

U. S. COPYRIGHT OFFICE, *Dramatic Compositions Copyrighted in the United States,* 1876, 1879. Listing of Locke's two plays.

WAGGONER, CLARK, ed. *History of the City of Toledo and Lucas County, Ohio.* New York: Munsell & Company, Publishers, 1888. Contains some biographical details on Locke.

Index

Index

Abbot, Francis Ellingwood, 42
Agassiz, Louis, 33
Agriculture, Locke's views of, 24
Alcohol, Locke's views of, 60-63
Alger, Horatio, 138-39

Beecher, Henry Ward, 117
Bellefontaine, Ohio, *Republican*, 27
Bible, Locke's references to, 95-96
Billings, Josh, *see* Shaw, Henry Wheeler
Bishop, Charles B., 42
Blaine, James G., 98
Bonner, Robert, 117
Bouton, Emily S., 56, 142
Boutwell, George S., 97
Brackenridge, Hugh Henry, 54
Brinkerhoff, Roeliff, 28, 29
Browne, Charles Farrar, 26, 65, 67-68, 89, 113, 140
Bryant, William Cullen, 94
Bucyrus, Ohio, *Journal*, 30-31
Burchard, Samuel Dickinson, 93
Burgess, Neil, 42, 111
Butler, Benjamin, 87

Cable, George Washington, 60
Chase, Salmon P., 29
Clemens, Cyril, 7
Clemens, Samuel L., 26, 36-38, 60, 99-100, 103, 109, 112-13, 116, 126, 129, 140, 147 (n. 21)
Cleveland, Grover, 86
Cobb, Sylvanus, Jr., 117
Corruption in government, Locke's views of, 53—54
Cortland, New York, *Democrat*, 20
Crever, J. A., 30

Davis, Jefferson, 82, 83, 86, 96
Democratic Party, 21, 26, 30, 41, 45, 50, 52, 53, 79, 91

Dialect, Locke's use of, 90-91
Dickens, Charles, 132
Dickinson, Anna E., 37
Dos Passos, John, 137
Douglas, Stephen A., 26, 45, 46
Downing, Jack, *see* Smith, Seba

Emancipation Proclamation, Locke's views of, 47, 75
Everett, Edward, 117

Findlay, Ohio, *Hancock Jeffersonian*, 32-34
Fountain of Temperance, Locke's temperance newspaper, 21
Franklin, Benjamin, 17, 19, 27, 65, 97, 139
Frémont, John C., 87
Ford, Harvey S., 7

Garfield, James A., 109
Gayler, Charles, 42, 109
Goldsmith, Oliver, 106
Gough, John B., 37
Grant, Ulysses S., 19, 41, 50, 52-53, 79, 119
Greeley, Horace, 41

Haight, Seth, 21
Hancock, Winfield S., 82
Harris, George Washington, 66, 68, 77
Harrison, John M., 8
Harte, Bret, 89
Hawthorne, Nathaniel, 118
Hayes, Rutherford B., 43, 53, 87-88
Hoadley, G. R., 61
Hooper, Johnson J., 25, 65, 68
Hunt, Leigh, 103

Immigration, Locke's views of, 58-59
The Index, 42

Irish, Locke's views of, 57-59, 100-2, 126

Irony, Locke's use of, 91

Jacksonianism, and Locke, 45
James, Henry, 103
Jefferson, Thomas, 113-15
Johnson, Andrew, 47-50, 80, 82, 86, 92, 117
Johnston, Robert, 39
Jones, Joseph, 7

Knights of the Golden Circle, Locke's opposition to, 31

Laissez faire, 44
Lee, Robert E., 96
Lincoln, Abraham, 19, 33-34, 46, 47, 83, 86, 98, 136
Locke, David Ross (Petroleum V. Nasby, *pseud.*): chronology, 11-13; birth, 19; childhood, 20; in Plymouth, Ohio, 22-28; marriage, 27; in Mansfield, Ohio, 28; in Bucyrus, Ohio, 30-32; fiction, 31; and Civil War, 31-32; in Findlay, Ohio, 32-34; Nasby letters, 33; in Toledo, Ohio, 34; description, 36-37; lecturer, 37-38; pamphlets, 38; publisher, 39; in New York, 39-41; dramatist, 42-43; death, 43; political views, 44-56; on women's rights, 56-57; on the Irish, 57-59; on temperance, 59-63; origins of Nasby, 65-77; Nasby, 77-98; plays, 109-11; lectures, 111-19; fiction, 120-40; achievement, 138-40; bibliography, 148-53

WRITINGS OF:

Androo Johnson, His Life, 38
Andy's Trip to the West, 48
Comic stories, 121-27
"Cussid Be Canaan," 113-16
The Demagogue, 38, 134-37
The Democratic John Bunyan, 38

The Diary of an Office Seeker, 38
Divers Views, Opinions, and Prophecies of Petroleum V. Nasby, 34
Ekkoes from Kentucky, 50
Elsey Farm, 128-29
Essay on Lincoln, 34
Hannah Jane, 38, 106-7
Hymns, 107-9
The Impendin Crisis uv the Democracy, 38
"In Search of the Man of Sin," 118-19
Inflation, 42, 109-10
Inflation at the Cross Roads, 38
John Duncan's Widow, 128-29
The Morals of Abou Ben Adhem, 38, 103-6
Nasby in Exile, 43, 99-103
Nasby letters, 33, 38, 64-98
The Nasby Letters, 88
The Nasby Papers, 34
Nasby's Life of Andy Jonsun, 48
A Paper City, 38, 130-32
The President's Policy, 38
"Prohibition" in *North American Review,* 62-63
Romances, 127-29
Sniggs letters, 28-29, 68-72, 141
Strong Heart and Steady Hand, 132-34
"The Struggles of a Conservative with the Woman Question," 116-17
The Struggles of Petroleum V. Nasby, 88
Swinging Round the Circle, 48
Swingin' Round the Cirkle, 49
Widow Bedott, 42, 109-11
Locke, Edmund (son), 28
Locke, Hester Ross (mother), 19
Locke, Martha Hannah Bodine (wife), 27
Locke, Nathaniel Reed (father), 19
Locke, Robinson (son), 27-28, 30, 43

Locke's National Monthly, 39
Lowell, James Russell, 64, 65, 66-67
Lovingood, Sut, *see* Harris, George
  Washington

Mansfield, Ohio, *Herald,* 28-30
McClellan, George B., 83, 86-87
McCune, Robert, 93
McElroy, John, 38, 51
Medary, Samuel, 29
Medill, Joseph, 29
Morrisey, John, 119

Nasby letters, 33-34, 64-98
Nasby, Petroleum V., *see* Locke,
  David Ross
Nast, Thomas, 37, 40-41
Negro rights, 50-51, 114-15
New York *Evening Mail,* 39-41
Nightingale, Florence, 33
Norris, Frank, 132

Paine, Thomas, 97
Palmer, Joseph, 42
Paper currency, Locke's views of,
  55-56
Pelton, Alonzo D., 34
Phillips, Wendell, 48
Pittsburgh *Post,* 26
Plymouth, Ohio, *Advertiser,* 22-27
Poe, Edgar Allan, 122
Power, Susan C. Dunning, 132
Prohibition, Locke's views of, 62-63

Redpath, James, 37, 59
Republican Party, 26, 29, 45-52,
  79, 114, 139
Robinson, James G., 22, 25, 26, 28,
  29, 30, 31, 120

Sarcasm, Locke's use of, 91-93
Scott, Walter, 129

Seymour, Horatio, 50
Shakespeare, William, 94
Shaw, Henry Wheeler, 37, 90, 113
Smith, Seba, 65, 66
Sons of Temperance, 21
Spear, S. A., 32
Stowe, Harriet Beecher, 97
Suggs, Simon, *see* Hooper, John-
  son J.
Sumner, Charles, 64
Swift, Jonathan, 96

Talmage, Thomas DeWitt, 56
Tammany Hall, 41, 52, 57, 119
Tariff, Locke's views of, 54-55
Tilden, Samuel J., 53-54, 82, 87-88,
  93
Toledo, Ohio, *Blade,* 34-35
Toledo, Ohio, Locke's investments
  in, 41-42
Toledo *Weekly Blade,* 35-36
Train, George Francis, 106
Twain, Mark, *see* Clemens, Sam-
  uel L.
Tweed Ring, 41, 52

Vallandigham, Clement C., 29, 81-
  83, 84, 86-87
Vanderbilt, Cornelius, 119

Ward, Artemus, *see* Browne,
  Charles F.
Warner, Charles Dudley, 109
Warren, Robert Penn, 137
Whitcher, Frances, 42, 109-10
Women's rights, 56-57, 116-17
Wood, Benjamin, 119
Wood, Fernando, 86-87, 119
Woodhull, Victoria Claflin, 106

Yost, G. W. N., 41